200· 710445

FAITH AND THE NATION

Kevin Williams

Faith &
the Nation

RELIGION, CULTURE
AND SCHOOLING
IN IRELAND

DOMINICAN PUBLICATIONS

First published (2005) by
Dominican Publications
42 Parnell Square
Dublin 1

ISBN 1-871552-94-X

British Library Cataloguing in Publications Data.
A catalogue record for this book is available
from the British Library.

Cover design by Bill Bolger

Printed in Ireland by
The Leinster Leader Ltd
Naas, Co. Kildare.

Contents

Foreword

Any book requires the help and forbearance of many people. I am grateful to Bernard Treacy and the editorial committee of Dominican Publications for their confidence in the project. Acknowledgment is also due to Dermot Lane, Michael Drumm and the Board of Mater Dei Institute for granting me sabbatical leave during which to write the book and to the Irish Research Council for the Humanities and Social Sciences for a grant that facilitated the research.

Many friends and colleagues in Mater Dei Institute and in Dublin City University and from other universities in Ireland and overseas offered scholarly, practical and moral support. I can name but a few but for their support in various ways at different stages in planning and writing this book, I am grateful to Caroline Renehan, James Norman, Paul Tighe, Eoin Cassidy, Colm Lennon, Gerry McNamara, Gerry Whyte, Declan Kiberd, David Carr, Eamonn Callan and Orla Kelly. Responsibility for any deficiencies in style or argument is entirely my own.

Most of all for their forbearance, interest and love, I thank my wife Fiona, and children Caitríona, Patrick and Áine.

INTRODUCTION

The Pursuit of Truth

Throughout the history of civilisation, religion, culture and schooling have been related. This relationship is to be found in the Jewish and Islamic traditions as well as within Christianity. In the Western tradition in both the monastic foundations of early Christian Ireland and in the cathedral schools of medieval Europe the pursuit of learning and praise of God went together. The commitments both to understand and to spread the Word of God were conceived as inseparable aspects of the Christian's mission.

At the time of the Reformation, on much of the European continent, Catholic and Protestant rulers assumed for themselves the teaching authority, the *auctoritas docendi*, which had hitherto been exercised by the papacy. Each ruler decided what was to be the religion of his region on the basis of *cuius regio, eius religio*. These rulers envisaged the authority to rule, to 'command for truth', and to educate as intimately linked and they used their newly appropriated authority to develop an educational infrastructure that would serve to promote a uniform cultural and religious identity among their inhabitants. The characterisation by John Knox of the city of Geneva under the rule of Calvin as a 'school' dramatically reflects the tendency to combine the educational and catechetical remits of governance.[1]

In the nineteenth century one of the most famous (or perhaps notorious) statements of the role of religion in schooling is conveyed in the words of Sir James Graham after the strike movements of 1842 (the Plug Riots): 'The police and soldiers have done their duty, the time is arrived when moral and religious instruction must go forth to reclaim the people from

---

1. See Michael Oakeshott, *On Human Conduct* (Oxford: Clarendon Press, 1975), p. 285.

the error of their ways'.[2] Significantly, the system of public schooling that developed in nineteenth century Britain was built up largely by the individual Churches.

Today educational policy-makers continue to define and give practical content to national identity and aspirations. The school curriculum still remains as an instrument of public policy through which national self-understanding is expressed and communicated to the young generation. But in the twenty-first century the notion of using the curriculum to promote a particular religious view of the world would be considered, in most liberal democracies, as an unacceptable encroachment of religion into the civic space.

In France, for example, the state school is conceived as a rigorously secular civic arena in which any expression of religious commitment is prohibited, including most controversially, the wearing of Islamic headscarves. As a consequence, even the teaching of history of religions or religious studies may be rejected as a Trojan horse designed to subvert the secular polity.[3] It can happen therefore that some young people never encounter even the religious dimension of culture in school contexts. This has led to both secularists and believers expressing concern at the religious illiteracy (*l'inculture religieuse* or *analphabétisme religieux*) of young people.[4]

The situation with regard to the place of religion in public schools in the United States is similar to that in France. The failure to accommodate the study of religion in the American curriculum also has also led to concern being expressed by philosophers of education. If religion is not studied in public schools, it is argued, then the education of young people is not

2. Cited in Richard Johnson, 'The Schooling of the English Working-Class, 1780-1850' in *Schooling and Capitalism*, eds. Roger Dale, Geoff Esland, and Madeleine MacDonald (London and Henley: Routledge and Kegan Paul/Open University Press, 1976), pp. 44-54, p. 50.

3. See Régis Debray, *L'Enseignement du Fait Religieux dans L'École Laïque*, (Paris: Editions Odile Jacob, 2002), p. 22. See also Alain Bost, *La Fin de l'État Laïc, Le Monde de L'Éducation*, no. 306 (septembre, 2002), p. 6.

4. Debray, *L'Enseignement du Fait Religieux dans L'École Laïque*, pp. 15, 39.

comprehensive nor does it equip young people to appraise truth claims in religion.[5]

By contrast, in the United Kingdom all schools have to promote spiritual and moral values, and daily worship and religious education are compulsory. But, as is common elsewhere, parents do enjoy the right to withdraw their children from religious education. A third approach is taken in Norway where a considered attempt is made to balance the secular and religious dimensions of cultural initiation. (The Norwegian approach will be considered in some detail in the Conclusion of this volume.) Whatever view is taken, every state has to define how it envisages religion having a place in a nation's culture as this is defined *via* its school curriculum.

Somewhat ironically, the involvement of the state in sponsoring schools in 1831 in Ireland was on the basis that their remit would be limited to secular learning and that provision for the teaching of religion was to be the responsibility of the respective Churches. This separation of secular and religious learning was rejected by the population. The Irish version of republicanism that was endorsed by the State from its foundation sought formally to integrate the secular and religious spheres of knowledge. This book illustrates, through an examination of selected documents, the role which, from its foundation in 1922, the new State attributed to education in promoting the Christian, specifically Catholic, identity of its young citizens. It also explores the attempts made by the State, especially from the 1990s, to distance itself from a direct role in reinforcing the religious dimension of cultural identity.

This distancing is a feature of a general tension between confessional and liberal elements in educational policy. This tension is expressed in an endeavour to reconcile respect for the nation's Christian heritage with respect for the other versions of human self-understanding, deriving from secular and from other

---

5. The current debate is the United States is examined in Suzanne Rosenblith and Scott Priestman, 'Problematizing Religious Truth: Implications for Public Education', *Educational Theory*, vol. 54, no. 4 (2004), pp. 365-380.

religious sources. This tension has a long history and is particularly prominent in the Green and White Papers of 1992 and 1995 respectively and in the Education Act of 1998. It is a tension that continues to characterise policy in the twenty-first century.

SOME MATTERS OF DEFINITION

Before offering an overview of how the volume is organised, a brief word about terminology is necessary. At least some of the disagreement about religion in education might be dispelled if people were clear about the terms used. What is offered here is a series of working definitions – they do not aspire to be exhaustive or comprehensive. Given that the subject is so complex and has many grey areas, it would be impossible to provide definitions that would cover everything or be completely acceptable to everyone.

Religious Education and Catechesis

Religious Education is taken to mean the teaching of religion and religious subject-matter with a view to informing and enlightening learners and does not presuppose religious faith on the part of teacher or learners. Although some learners may come to have their commitment to a faith reinforced, this is not the purpose of Religious Education. Catechesis is a sub-set of Religious Education and it means teaching religion with the added purpose of developing Christian faith. Catechesis can therefore be described as formative in intent, although not all of those who study in a catechetical context become or remain convinced believers. In Ireland the teaching of religion was historically referred to as Religious Instruction, understood as teaching of a catechetical nature.

Kinds of School

The terms 'confessional', 'denominational' or 'faith' schools are taken to be synonymous. Firstly, there are confessional, or more accurately mono-confessional, schools. These aim, as a matter of policy, to foster in young people a commitment to a particular religion and the religion in question is reinforced as part of the school's ethos. Schools can be mono-confessional in respect of management and trusteeship/patronage but accept a confessionally-mixed student population and, indeed, make no faith requirements of teachers or even of the principal.

Secondly, there are inter-faith or ecumenical schools. Within these school some core, shared religious beliefs are accepted and promoted as part of the school's ethos but religious faith is not associated with a single religious faith or denomination. Ecumenical schools may offer an agreed syllabus of a catechetical character or they may provide confessional religious education to the children of those parents who request it. The essential point is that religious education is provided during the normal school day within the timetabled curriculum.

A third category consists of schools that, in Ireland, have traditionally been referred to as multi-denominational. Based on a principle of equal inclusion, these cater for children from all religious backgrounds and from none. The values of tolerance rather than any religious belief define the ethos of these schools. Within the timetabled curriculum, pupils are taught about worldviews with the aim of fostering tolerance and respect for different traditions in the context of promoting an agreed set of moral principles. The annual festivals and sacred days of different religious groups represented in the school are marked and celebrated. Provision for denominationally-specific religious instruction for those pupils whose parents who seek it, is made outside schools hours.

Fourthly, there are what can be described as non-denominational or secular schools. These are based on a principle of equal exclusion. In France, for example, the state school is conceived as religion-free space and all teaching of religion even as a cultural, sociological or psychological phenomenon is prohibited. But all secular schools, even those where the study of religion as a human phenomenon is accommodated, normally preclude within school hours, even as an option, catechetical religious education in the sense of the fostering of religious belief and practice

Ethos

As the term 'ethos' arises often in these discussions, let me say something about it. Our current understanding of the term 'ethos' reflects very strongly the Greek genesis of the word as character or disposition. Every human institution has its own ethos in the sense of a dominant, pervading spirit or character that finds expression in the habits of behaviour of those who are part of it. As well as in schools, ethos can be identified in political parties, hospitals, sports bodies, trades unions and in every place of work. An ethos sometimes has a religious connotations but this is a contingent rather than a necessary aspect of the concept. In other words, ethos need not, in principle, imply anything religious.

Let us next turn to the structure of the book.

OVERVIEW OF CHAPTERS

Chapter One deals with the relationship between faith and culture but it is not intended as an exhaustive, scholarly account of this relationship. It is rather a snapshot of the relationship with reference both to Ireland and to other cultures. Following a brief survey of historical background, the second chapter considers the policy of the Irish State towards the religious formation of its citizens from 1922 until the 1970s. The third chapter examines the liberal challenge to this policy and traces the government's response to this challenge in the policy documents of the 1990s, including the Education Act of 1998. In Chapter Four, the impact of government policy for the changed climate with regard to the teaching of religion at second level is explored. Chapter Five examines in detail the new primary curriculum and Chapter Six teases out an approach that might reconcile the conflicting demands of respect for tradition and openness to diversity in primary schools. The volume concludes with a tentative evocation of the inclusive spirit of Christian Ireland in the twenty-first century.

The major focus of the book is on the role that the Irish state, through the educational system, has adopted and continues to adopt towards promoting religious identity. I am aware of the different configuration of schooling and of the different tradition in religious education in Northern Ireland and the situation there merits a volume in its own right. This book explores the relationship between faith and the state as mediated through the education system in the southern part of the island. Based on an analysis of the educational system as it has developed, the book is not concerned to advance an argument about the patronage, control or management of schools.

I am well aware that any treatment of the relationship between religion and education in Ireland, and indeed in most other countries, most notably perhaps in France and in the USA, tends to prompt polarised attitudes and a tendency to see things in stark either/or terms. The strong feelings that this issue provokes have historically had a wide impact on political life generally and they continue to influence modern politics.[6] In dealing with this topic a writer should, above all, aspire to avoid what novelist, Ian McEwan, refers to as 'that old business of theorising, taking up a position, planting the flag of identity and self-esteem, then fighting all comers to the end'.[7]

The arguments advanced in the book are based on realism and common sense and derive from three related commitments. These are commitments to our Christian heritage, to liberal democratic principles, and to the need for a shared civic culture. I am aware that some readers will find that the arguments are too concerned to affirm the claims of the Christian tradition, while others will find that I am too concerned to respond to the claims of diversity. Such criticism is often the lot of writers who do not

6. There is a very good account of the impact of the faith and schools debate on political life historically and in the present in three countries in Harry Judge, *Faith-based schools and the State: Catholics in America, France and England* (Oxford: Symposium Book, 2002). The intense feelings that the issue of control of schooling can prompt in the Northern Irish context is well documented in Finnuala O'Connor, *A Shared Childhood: The Story of Integrated Schools in Northern Ireland* (Belfast: Blackstaff Press, 2002). A recent study visit to Spain brought home to me also how changes of government involve changes in the profile of religion in education in this country.

7. Ian McEwan, *The Child in Time* (London: Picador, 1998), p. 80.

offer total support to particular attitudes and policies. To critics in both categories, I would say that we inhabit the corner of the universe in which we find ourselves rather than a perfect world where the wishes of all can be met to the complete satisfaction of everyone.

THE INTERDISCIPLINARY SPIRIT

I am a philosopher by trade and training but this volume is interdisciplinary in character, dealing as it does with philosophical, historical and legal aspects of policy documents on education. The issues raised here have an important sociological dimension but adequate exploration of this dimension would require another book.[8]

What may surprise some readers is that, in order to communicate some of the concrete, lived sense of the subject-matter, the book also draws, where relevant, on literary texts – poetry, fiction and biography. This approach is consistent with an important Irish intellectual tradition identified by the distinguished Irish philosopher, William Desmond. He argues that in the past in Ireland 'the fields of articulation were dominated, on the one hand, by the poets, who have a long and august tradition as well as commanding some audience, and, on the other hand, by the religious ascendancy of the Catholic Church'.[9] In discussing the relationship between faith and culture and education, literary sources can enhance understanding greatly because they prevent the discussion being conducted at a level of high theory that connects little with the lived experience of human beings.

The difference between abstract theory and literature as conduits of human understanding is captured in Goethe's distinction between theory and life itself: 'Grey, dear friend, is theory all / And green the golden tree of life' ('*Grau, theurer*

8. For a recent survey text, readers should consult Hilary Tovey and Perry Share, *A Sociology of Ireland*, second edition (Dublin: Gill and Macmillan, 2003). The volume contains extensive sections on both religion and education, with analysis of research in the area.

9. Jason J. Howard, 'Interview with William Desmond', *The Leuven Philosophy Newsletter*, Vol. 2 (2002), pp. 15-19, p. 19.

freund, ist alle theorie, / Und grün des Lebens goldener Baum).[10] Of necessity there is a greyness in some philosophical and historical work but literature does offer something of the 'green' of life's 'golden tree'. Images remain with us long after facts and theories have dropped into the great well of human forgetfulness. Although theory is unavoidable, there is also a sense in which, in discussions of human practices, it is wise to keep the theoretical at arm's length. In its modest way, this volume endeavours to offer a kind of reflection that is 'as rich and concrete' as poetry and 'as serious about what is ultimate' as philosophy and religion.[11] In any case, the use of literature in search of understanding is consistent with the pursuit of the Dominican motto, *Veritas*. As John McGahern puts i,t 'fiction is a very serious thing, that while it is fiction, it is also a revelation of truth, or facts'.[12]

With these words in mind, let us turn then to an exploration of the relationship between faith and culture.

10. Quoted in R. Grant, *Thinkers of Our Time: Oakeshott* (The Claridge Press: London, 1990), p. 118. I have slightly changed Grant's translation.

11. Howard, 'Interview with William Desmond', p. 19

12. Eamon Maher, 'An Interview with John McGahern: Catholicism and National Identity in the Works of John McGahern', *Studies: An Irish Quarterly Review*, vol. 90, no. 357 (Spring 2001), pp. 70-83, p. 74.

CHAPTER ONE

Faith and Culture

In what is perhaps the outstanding Flemish novel of the twentieth century, *The Sorrow of Belgium*, by Hugo Claus, the grandfather of protagonist, Louis, possesses a tailor-made suit from Ireland that he greatly prizes. Before being ironed the suit is sprinkled with holy water in honour of the suit's provenance from that 'land of missionaries and marytrs'.[1]

This perception of Ireland reflects the salience of religion in Irish life. Historian Colm Lennon has described the intimate connection between Irish culture and Christianity as an expression of the 'seamlessness of the sacred and secular spheres' in Irish life.[2] In this chapter, the relationship between faith and culture is examined both in Ireland and internationally. The first section aims to show how initiation into a culture can involve initiation into a religion. The second demonstrates how initiation into a religion can *pari passu* involve assimilation of a culture.[3]

THE RELATIONSHIP BETWEEN CULTURE AND RELIGION

The Irish language is the pre-eminent vehicle of the relationship between faith and culture in Ireland. Perception of this relationship prompted the famous comments from Eamon De Valera that the language is 'the bearer to us of a philosophy, of an outlook on life deeply Christian and rich in practical wis-

---

1. Hugo Claus, *The Sorrow of Belgium*, translated by Arnold J. Pomerans (Woodstock and New York: The Overlook Press, 2002), p. 507.

2. Colm Lennon, *Sixteenth Century Ireland: The Incomplete Conquest* (Dublin: Gill and Macmillan, 1994), p. 133.

3. I consider some of the passages explored here from the point of view of their implications for understanding the relationship between faith and culture in an increasing secularised world in Kevin Williams, 'The Religious Dimension of Cultural Initiation: Has It a Place in a Secular World?', *Ethical Perspectives*, vol. 11, no. 4 (December 2004), pp. 238-237.

dom'.[4] The language illustrates very clearly what has been called a 'ghostly rhythm'[5] in Irish culture where the 'seamlessness of the sacred and secular' is very obvious. Idioms which make reference to God are quite common. *Dia dhuit, Dia's Muire dhuit, Dia's Muire dhuit 's Pádraig* and *Beannacht Dé ort* are everyday salutations (similar to *Grüss Gott* used in parts of the German-speaking world and *Namasté* in Hindi). The invocations of God have a reality in these idioms which is certainly lost in the English 'good-bye' and the Spanish *adíos*. Even in Irish there are words such as the days of the week *An Chéadaoin, Déardaoin* and *An Aoine* meaning 'first fast', 'middle fast', and 'fast' which have lost their liturgical significance. To be sure, there are many common expressions such as *buíochas le Dia, le cúnamh Dé, bail ó Dhia ar an obair* or *go cumhdaí Dia sibh* which can be replaced by secular idioms – just as it is possible to avoid using the expression *Grüss Gott*, with its religious connotations. But only in informal greetings can an Irish-speaker, believer or atheist, avoid the reference to God in *Dia dhuit*.

The theological orientation of this mindset is also tellingly evoked in the use of the wonderfully sensitive term *duine le Dia* to describe a person who is learning disabled.

As in Italy and in the Spanish- and Portuguese-speaking worlds, the Virgin Mary has a very prominent profile in Ireland. This is expressed in the use of a special word, *Muire*, to refer to the Virgin Mary that is distinct from the Christian name, *Máire*. Its use in the term *Muire na nGael* suggests something of special place attributed to Mary in Irish culture.

The 'ghostly rhythm' of the language with its orientation to God does not lend itself to certain changes. Recently I have noted that some secular English-speakers who are having their children educated through Irish use the totally non-Irish expression,

---

4. Eamon De Valera, Radio broadcast (17 March 1943). http://www.searcs-web.com/dev.html. Accessed 10 July 2004.

5. The expression 'ghostly rhythms' is adapted from John McGahern by Bruce Bradley. See B. Bradley, 'Ghostly Rhythms: Philosophy and Religion in Irish Education', *Studies: An Irish Quarterly Review*, vol. 83, no. 330 (1994), pp. 143-152.

maidin maith, which is about as appropriate as translating '*Bon appétit*' as 'Good appetite'. It would in fact be less alien to Irish culture to say 'Hi' or 'Hello'.

The 'ghostly rhythm' that gives expression to a religious worldview can assert itself almost unselfconsciously. At a seminar on Relationships and Sexuality Education that I once attended, a representative of the Department of Education and Science in Ireland gave an impeccably liberal, neutral and sensitive address on the subject. Yet in a later presentation in Irish on the same theme, sexual intercourse was referred to as *an gníomh giniúna* (the procreative or generative act). This implicit endorsement of a Catholic view on sexuality was entirely absent in English. A Catholic orientation to moral theology was communicated *via* the language the speaker used rather than because she believed that every sexual act must be open to the transmission of life.

But it would be a mistake to think that an intimate relationship between culture and religion is to be found only in Ireland.

PERSPECTIVES FROM AFRICA AND ITALY

In her novel, *The Poisonwood Bible,* Barbara Kingsolver gives fictional expression to the manner in which sensitivity to religious sensibility can be required to engage with some African cultures.

An American family arrives in the Congo in the early 1960s because the father wishes to pursue his mission of evangelising the natives. The father, Reverend Price, is unable to make any kind of imaginative connection with African culture. He subscribes to a rigid and stern Protestantism that makes no allowance for any deviation from a strict theological and moral code. Failing entirely to display any understanding of, or sympathy towards, native religion and culture, he is unable to comprehend the antagonism displayed by the natives towards Christianity. When informed that the village chief is worried that he is trying to 'lure' the villagers into 'following corrupt ways' and leading them 'down into a hole, where they may fail to see the proper sun and become trapped like bugs on a rotten carcass', he attributes the chief's concern to perverseness on his part.[6] His attitude is contrasted with that of Brother Fowles, Reverend Price's predecessor as missionary, who has gone native and has even married a Congolese. He has 'come to love the people here and their ways of thinking'[7] and he resonates to their sense of religion which he explains as follows:

> 'Everything they do is with one eye to the spirit. When they plant their yams and manioc, they're praying. When they harvest, they're praying. Even when they conceive their children, I think they're praying ... I think the Congolese have a world of God's grace in their lives ... '.[8]

Christian missionaries, he explains, were, not required to teach them to pray and worship because 'they already knew how to make a joyful noise unto the Lord a long time ago ... They're very worshipful. It's a grand way to begin a church service, singing a Congolese hymn to the rainfall on the seed yams'.[9]

Father Jack in Brian Friel's play, *Dancing at Lughnasa*, is another example of a fictional character for whom identifying with his congregation meant appropriating its religious worldview.

Another literary illustration of the relationship between religion and cultural initiation is to be found in novelist Tim Parks's account, *An Italian Education,* of his experience as a parent of three young children growing up in Italy. Although Parks does not believe in God, he retains his Anglo-Saxon, Protestant cultural and moral presuppositions. Parks exercises the parental right to withdraw his children from religion class but it takes him some time in Italy to appreciate that withholding his children from sacramental preparation and religious class is perceived as an expression of 'churlish' pride.[10] What he has done is to exclude the children from the community for the sake of 'dubi-

---

6. Barbara Kingsolver, *The Poisonwood Bible* (London: Faber and Faber, 1999), pp. 146-7.

7. Ibid., p. 280

8. Ibid., p. 278

9. Ibid.

10. Tim Parks, *An Italian Education* (London: Vintage, 2000), p. 220.

ous notions of sincerity and coherence'.[11]

Moreover, the exemption of his children from religious instruction in school has not immunised them against religious influence. At first, all who were withdrawn from religion were due to do Peace Studies but this was subsequently changed to a version of European Studies called *Osservazione all'Europa.* However, in these classes one of the first things the pupils learn is that what unites European nations is Roman Catholicism, the religion of Italian people.[12]

Just as religion can be part of a culture, initiation into a religion can *pari passu* involve assimilation of a culture. The place of religion in cultural formation is reflected in the folk distinction between Catholic atheists and Protestant atheists. Let us therefore consider how religious and cultural socialisation are linked.

RELIGIOUS AND CULTURAL SOCIALISATION

The first example I take is from Mary McCarthy who, although not Irish, was brought up in a Chicago environment that was deeply pervaded by Irish Catholicism. Few writers have captured more tellingly the great cultural loading that can accompany a religious upbringing than this American novelist. I would point out that McCarthy rejected the religious beliefs of her childhood and came to assume a very critical attitude towards the philosophical basis of Christianity and towards moral aspects of religion in general and of Catholicism in particular. Yet she retains a positive attitude towards the education she received, one that would not be shared by all past pupils of Catholic schools.[13]

Perhaps I should also say, reflecting on my own experience of a Catholic education, that its impact on an intelligent and sensitive person like Mary McCarthy is unlikely to be replicated

11. Ibid.
12. Ibid., pp.. 248-250, 288.
13 See, for example, Jackie Bennett and Rosemary Forgan, eds., *Convent Girls* (London: Virago Press, 2003).

in the lives of young people who are intellectually less able and less culturally informed.

For McCarthy though, the general cultural benefits of a Catholic upbringing were considerable. She is 'not sorry to have *been* a Catholic' and among the very 'practical reasons' that she gives are the advantages of knowing Latin and the stories of the saints.[14]. When later in life she came to study Latin, it was, she writes, 'easy for me and attractive, too, like an old friend'.[15] She explains that it can be useful to know the lives of the saints in order to understand, for example, the meaning of the name Agnes and why it is associated with a lamb or that a tooth is the symbol for Saint Apollonia who is the patron saint of dentists or why the martyrdom of Saint Catherine of Alexandria is associated with a wheel.

McCarthy then raises the manner in which religious, indeed, theological concerns can be an integral part of understanding poetry. When adult readers have to study some theology in order to read the English Metaphysical poets it is 'like being taught the Bible as Great Literature in a college humanities course; it does not stick to the ribs'.[16] She claims that most American students 'have no other recourse than to take these vitamin injections to make good the cultural deficiency'.[17] The potency of a religious education is strikingly communicated in the image of 'sticking to the ribs'. By contrast, the image of taking 'vitamins injections to make good cultural deficiency' vividly conveys the consequence of excluding the study of religion from schools.

But the Catholic faith was not taught as a vehicle for imparting culture; the promotion of collateral cultural learning was not in the minds of her teachers. For them the idea that young people would study theology or Church history for its cultural benefits would have seemed 'atrocious blasphemy'.[18] Religious purposes

14 Mary McCarthy, *Memories of a Catholic Girlhood* (Harmondworth, London: Penguin, 1967), p. 24.
  15. Ibid.
  16. Ibid.
  17. Ibid.
  18. Ibid, p. 26.

dominated the educational outlook of the teachers and any other cultural enrichment was purely incidental.

Just as the political and cultural identity of many Irish people has been associated with religion, so too was that of Mary McCarthy. A Catholic education, she argues, involved the absorption of a perspective on world history and ideas before even the end of primary school. The 'indelible' effect of this process was 'like learning a language early'.[19] The Catholic perspective, she acknowledges, was, indeed, biased but its advantage from the learners' point of view was that it was not 'dry or dead' and that it brought history alive 'by the violent partisanship' which informed it.[20]

Another effect of this partisanship was to introduce a coherence into the students' conception of history because the perspectivism acted as a 'magnet'[21] that brought information together into a single conceptual framework. Catholic school history in the USA also required the learning of English and French history in such fine detail that 'the past of a foreign country ... [became] one's own'.[22] This education was not merely a matter of accumulating more extensive quantities of information. It was a question of knowledge becoming 'a part of oneself' and becoming also 'a matter of feeling'.[23] This derived from caring deeply about the past and from identifying 'passionately' with the cause of faith.[24]

The fact that the struggle for Catholic hegemony was a 'losing cause' prompted a rebellious nonconformity against the prevailing political establishment.[25] In this respect Catholic children had a different attitude from other American children who were taught 'as though history had achieved a happy ending in American civics'.[26] In this passage the analogy of her Catholic

19. Ibid, p. 25.
20. Ibid.
21. Ibid.
22. Ibid.
23. Ibid.
24. Ibid.
25. Ibid.
26. Ibid.

upbringing with language learning is noteworthy because it communicates the intimacy of religious identity as 'part of oneself'. McCarthy's account could be considered an elaboration on the attitude of Germaine Greer who writes: 'I am still a Catholic, I just don't believe in God ... I don't want to escape from it. I'm very glad to be Catholic'.[27]

A memorable and positive image of the cultural loading that can be assumed by initiation into a religion is evoked in Chinua Achebe's novel, *Things Fall Apart*. Exhibiting an openness to the new, a young man, Nwoye, becomes 'captivated' by Christianity.[28] His embracing of this new religion is prompted not by the 'mad logic of the Trinity' but by the 'poetry' of the new religion – which he 'felt in the marrow'.[29] The words of his favourite hymn 'poured into his parched soul ... like the drops of frozen rain melting on the dry plate of the panting earth'.[30] Becoming a Christian involved an aesthetic as well as a religious experience.

An interesting image of the cultural dimension of religion, this time with particular reference to Catholicism, is offered by television journalist Anne Robinson in a reminiscence on her convent education. 'Catholicism', she writes, 'is not a religion, it's a nationality. I think that we are always, always, Catholics'.[31] Her former school principal may not consider that she is a Catholic but, writes Robinson, 'I know I'm a Catholic. If I bang my toe, I will suddenly say "Jesus, Mary and Joseph"!'[32]

The analogy between nationality and religion is interesting. Although a person may repudiate allegiance to a particular state by repudiating citizenship, the situation with regard to national identity is different. This is because national identity, as part of human self-understanding, is not normally something which one can decide to adopt or renounce at will. Although it is possible to reject particular versions of national identity (for

27. Bennett and Forgan, *Convent Girls*, pp. 103-4.
28. Chinua Achebe, *Things Fall Apart* (London: Heinemann, 1986), p. 106.
29. Ibid.
30. Ibid.
31. Bennett and Forgan, *Convent Girls*, pp. 171.
32. Ibid., p. 171-2.

example the association of Irishness with Catholicism or of Jewishness with Zionism), the culture of the national community into which one is born is part of one's very identity and so it cannot be renounced without leaving its residue. James Joyce, for example, who chose to live in exile and who trenchantly renounced his native land, remained culturally and psychologically very much an Irishman.

The point is well made by Louis MacNeice. In a poem dealing with his Irish identity, MacNeice writes that it is impossible for him to be '[a]nyone else than what this land engendered...'. He envisages his 'self' as being 'wed' to his past and consequently as a 'woven figure' that cannot be unravelled.[33]

By contrast with a national identity, a person may reject religious belief completely, as did James Joyce. Yet Anne Robinson's image does suggest that a religious identity can also be very pervasive and that the effects of a religious upbringing may not be readily discarded.

A lovely irony of the use of the nationality metaphor with regard to Catholicism is that the faith is completely international in its mission and compass. For a Catholic, as Marina Warner puts it, 'you belong to the world in an interesting way', a way that tends 'to transcend local nationalism'.[34]

IRISH PERSPECTIVES

Irish writers have frequently explored the intertwining of religion and culture. Bryan MacMahon captures much that is positive in this relationshi. Religious belief, for MacMahon, is a 'cultural treasure-house'.[35] He perceives the Catholic Church 'not alone as vehicle for my faith but as a fruitful source of my culture' and considers that 'the turning year is meaningless if not viewed through the focused lens of Christianity'.[36] In his profes-

33. From Louis MacNeice, 'Valediction' in Patricia Craig (ed.), *The Oxford Book of Ireland* (Oxford: Oxford University Press, 1999), pp. 357-9.
34. Bennett and Forgan, *Convent Girls*, p. 196.
35. Bryan MacMahon, *The Master* (Dublin: Poolbeg, 1992), p. 101.
36. Ibid., p. 1000.

sional work, the school year took its shape from the liturgical year. The feast-days punctuated the rhythm of school life and indeed in most Irish schools they still do.[37] For example, St Brigid's Day, Ash Wednesday, St Patrick's Day, Easter, Hallow E'en and Christmas all bring their own colour and excitement. Listening to stories and legends, weaving crosses, receiving ashes, designing cards, singing hymns and other songs, participating in school plays are among the activities that for children mark these moments in the year. Christmas traditions bring a special magic and delight and illuminate the dark days of winter.

He writes with regret but without bitterness of the emphasis in the past on the verbal formulae of religious belief and the 'rigidity of faith'.[38] At the time, he observes, his 'mind resembled a pair of binoculars held the wrong way around' and this meant that his religion appeared largely 'as something miniaturised, the details reduced to remoteness, coldness and abstraction'.[39] Through encounters with the 'liberation of literature', he was, fortunately, enabled 'to turn the binoculars the right way around' and thus encounter 'the dimensions of the Christian experience in forms far more spacious'.[40] This perception prompts him to plead for more emphasis to be put on 'the real beauty of the word of God'[41] and on the aesthetic and cultural dimensions of religion.

Like others too I have been struck by the acknowledgement made by John McGahern of the legacy bequeathed him by Irish Catholicism. Although now an unbeliever, he tells us that 'the Church was the most powerful thing in my upbringing, in the spiritual and cultural sense; much more powerful than literature which was almost absent. It dealt with the Mystery which nobody else dealt with. The society was basically against the Mystery.'[42]

37. Ibid., pp. 106/7.
38. Ibid., p. 100.
39. Ibid. p. 100.
40. Ibid.
41. Ibid., p. 106.
42. See Daniel Murphy, *Education and the Arts* (Dublin: School of Education, Trinity College, Dublin, 1987), p. 141.

In this upbringing, the Church, he comments, was 'the only cultural constant'.[43] In the absence of books and of 'hardly any manners, the ceremonies of the Church were certainly the most beautiful things'.[44] He refers here and elsewhere to the incident where Proust objected to attempts to remove the local *curé* from the town committee, 'if for nothing but the spire of his church which lifts men's eyes from the avaricious earth'.[45] Just in the way the iconography of medieval churches was the Bible of the poor, the Church was, he remarks, 'my first book and I would think it is still my most important book ... The only pictures we could see were religious pictures, the stations of the Cross. The only music we would hear was religious hymns'.[46] The Church introduced him to 'all I came to know of ceremony, even of luxury – the tulips that used to come in the flat boxes when I was an altar boy, the candles, the incense'.[47]

As well as being his first book, the Church was also his 'first fiction'.[48] As noted in the Introduction to this book, McGahern takes fiction very seriously in that 'while it is fiction, it is also a revelation of truth, or facts'.[49] Regarding Church teaching on the afterlife, he notes that '[w]e absolutely believed in Heaven and Hell, Purgatory and even Limbo. I mean they were actually closer to us than Australia or Canada ... they were real places'.[50]

Religion had a similar effect in the upbringing of Brendan Kennelly in Kerry of the 1940s. The Catholicism of the time, writes Kennelly, 'got me at the totally imagistic level of actually seeing things'.[51] What he finds very striking in retrospect is the

43. Ibid., p. 142.
44. Ibid.
45. Eamon Maher, 'An Interview with John McGahern: Catholicism and National Identity in the Works of John McGahern', *Studies*, vol. 90. no. 357 (Spring, 2001), pp. 70-83, p. 76. A slightly different version of this comment is in Murphy, *Education and the Arts,* p. 142.
46. Maher, 'An Interview with John McGahern', p. 72.
47. Ibid.
48. Ibid., p. 74.
49. Ibid.
50. Ibid.
51. All the quotations from Brendan Kennelly in this paragraph are taken from Murphy, *Education and the Arts*, pp. 48-56, p. 53.

sense 'that your whole moral being could be expressed in those terms, that everything you could feel or aspire to or know can be expressed in these extraordinary images of devils and angels, saints, Heaven, Hell, Purgatory and Limbo'.[52] He goes on to argue that these 'wonderful words ... never leave' a person who is 'filled' with them when young because their influence runs at 'very deep levels' in the human psyche.[53] Dividing 'the world into heroes and villains', this version of Catholicism offered 'a deliberate and melodramatic over-simplification of just about everything'.[54]

Catholicism's sense of closeness to the afterlife provides an orientation towards a world beyond the preoccupations of everyday life. This orientation of a religious upbringing is memorably captured by Mary McCarthy. '[T]ogether with much that proved to be practical', as we have just seen, McCarthy's education opened her mind to 'a conception of something prior to and beyond utility' in the spirit of the gospel exhortation to consider the lilies of the field or in the spirit of Mary Magdalen's anointing of Jesus' feet with alabaster anointment.[55] Through its architecture and art, whose richness often contrasted with the poverty of the faithful, the Church sanctioned what would appear to outsiders as 'sheer wastefulness'.[56] Wasteful too, in the eyes of many outsiders, were the lives of contemplative religious and their disregard for material gain. Like John McGahern, she recalls with gratitude the sense of 'mystery and wonder'[57] evoked through the Church's liturgies and ceremonies. Participation in these ceremonies could prompt 'exalted moments of altruism' when 'the soul was fired with reverence'.[58]

Let me continue with some other images that communicate the power of a religious upbringing to inform an individual's life.

52. Ibid.
53. Ibid.
54. Ibid.
55. McCarthy, *Memories of a Catholic Girlhood*, p. 26.
56. Ibid.
57. Ibid.
58. Ibid.

The first is from an interview with a Newfoundlander called Andy O'Brien about growing up in the Irish-Canadian community there. The children used to walk to their local school, St Patrick's. And religion was, 'of course', he states, 'the bone and sinew of our lives'.[59] The closeness of the divine in the secular could hardly be more vividly articulated.

In his autobiography, *Another Country: Growing up in '50s Ireland*, Gene Kerrigan writes of the Catholic Church that it 'permeated every pocket of our lives' although, he continues wryly, 'we knew little or nothing about religion'.[60] This is because the language of the theology of the time was incomprehensible to a child – as Bryan MacMahon has recorded so regretfully. Yet the religion of Gene Kerrigan's childhood was 'suspended by a massive web of devotional trappings, singly and in concert, designed to tether the sinner not to a religion but to the Church, weaving the Church into the very flesh and sinews of the community'.[61] The metaphor of 'sinew' used by Andy O'Brien re-appears but the overall effect of the imagery here is negative. Weaving, web and tethering evoke a system of beliefs that was imposed from the outside rather than embraced joyfully from within.

By contrast, poet Paul Durcan captures in a memorable image what is positive in Catholicism, although in the context of a critical attitude towards aspects of the institutional church. The image occurs at the end of a beautiful passage where he evokes his childhood as an altar server in Gonzaga when he 'used love cycling the empty Dublin streets in the pre-dawn darkness' and 'loved serving Mass'.[62] The holy sacramental quiet of these moments and the associated ritual are communicated in fond detail, and the passage concludes:

Irish Christianity was the mother tongue of my soul and it

59. Mary Russell, 'Lost and Found Land', *The Irish Times Magazine, 15* March 2003, pp. 14-15, p. 14.
60. Gene Kerrigan, *Another Country: Growing up in '50s Ireland* (Dublin: Gill and Macmillan, 1998), p. 102.
61. Ibid., p. 108.
62. Paul Durcan, *Paul Durcan's Diary* (Dublin: New Island, 2003), p. 120.

remains the mother tongue of my soul in spite of the institution of the Irish Roman Catholic Church.[63]

The use of the language metaphor here is striking and it echoes its use by McCarthy and also the use of the same metaphor for the same purposes by Marina Warner.[64] The metaphor captures very powerfully the intimacy of the connection between faith and culture. And, as we have seen, the theological orientation of Irish makes the relationship between language, culture and religion more than metaphorical in Ireland.

As the cultural identity of many Irish people has been associated with religion, does all of this mean that the Irish must inescapably come to see their national identity in religious terms? Of course not. Let me make more explicit a distinction, raised earlier in this chapter, between religion as culture and religion as belief. Like Leopold Bloom in Joyce's *Ulysses*, people can negotiate cultures without embracing their religious beliefs. This process is wryly captured in Polish-American author Eva Hoffman's recollection that her secular, Jewish mother when exasperated used to say 'Jesus, Joseph, and Sainted Maria'.[65] The expression was part of the culture and its use reflected neither belief in Christianity nor belief in God. Hoffman's encounter with the Catholicism of Poland no more secured a transition to religious faith than did James Joyce's Jesuit education.[66]

Novelist Isabel Allende makes a similar point about the role of Catholicism in the psyche of Chileans. No one, she claims, refers to herself or himself as an atheist, preferring to use instead the term agnostic. Even convinced non-believers seek religious consolation on their deathbeds on the grounds that a last Confession 'never hurt anyone'.[67] Significantly, too, she notes that the

63. Ibid., p. 121.

64. Bennett and Forgan (eds.), *Convent Girls*, p. 195.

65. Eva Hoffman, *Lost In Translation: A Life in a New Language* (London: Vintage, 1998), p. 30.

66. See Williams, 'The Religious Dimension of Cultural Initiation: Has It a Place in a Secular World?', p. 232.

67. Isabel Allende, *My Invented Country: A Memoir* (London: Harper Perennial, 2004), p. 58

profile of the Church in Chile has been enhanced by admiration of its role in defending the poor and of the courage and self-sacrifice of the priests and nuns who opposed the régime of Pinochet. Allende herself rejected religion entirely at fifteen but has failed to shake off its cultural residue by virtue of her tendency to pray and to make the sign of the cross in times of need.[68]

Likewise, although they live in a country where Christianity is deeply inculturated, Irish people do not have to be born or to remain Christian. Whether in anger, like James Joyce, or in sorrow like John McGahern, some will come to reject Christian belief. Yet the attitudes to life of Irish people are shaped by the religion that is a prominent feature of the culture in which they grow up. The embeddedness of religion in Irish culture means that an encounter with religion is not something that can normally be avoided. As a result, individuals have to choose what their attitude will be to religious belief which, rather than being relegated to the strictly private sphere, enjoys a profile in the nation's culture. Although religious belief can be accepted or rejected, religious sensibility is a salient feature of Irish culture.

But this does not mean that the state should seek to promote a connection between religion and identity. And, as we shall see, this is what happened when the faith-culture relationship was affirmed and promulgated as government policy.

68. Ibid., p. 61-63.

CHAPTER TWO

Shaping the Nation[1]

In the 1960s, when she was about fourteen, the girls in Olivia O'Leary's class in St Leo's convent in Carlow were asked what they thought of the new Mass in Irish. O'Leary expressed strong criticisms and found herself severely reprimanded for being 'unpatriotic'[2]: the impudent teenager had just attacked the two pillars of Irish identity, the Irish language and the Catholic Church. In the minds of the nuns of the time nationhood and Catholicism went together.

This conjunction runs very deeply in Irish people and can take surprising forms. For example, in an essay entitled 'Republic is a Beautiful Word', Roddy Doyle, an atheist who dislikes Pope John Paul II intensely, writes with bewilderment of his warm and positive reaction to seeing the Pope meet the Irish soccer team before the World Cup quarter final in Italy in 1990. When the Pope met the team, 'I couldn't fight down the lump in my throat as the lads in their tracksuits lined up to meet him. They were all Catholics, the reporter told us. Great, I thought; and I wasn't messing. It was strange'.[3] This response captures something of the resonance between the Catholic religion and national iden-tity in the Irish psyche. In Ireland the strong association between the Catholic Church and the struggle for independence has contributed to a close identification between loyalty to the nation and loyalty to the Church. The nationalist or republican tradition in Ireland is very different from the republicanism of

1 A previous version of this chapter appeared under the title 'Faith and the Nation: education and religious identity in the Republic of Ireland' in the *British Journal of Educational Studies*, vol. 47, no 4 (December 1999), pp. 317-331.

2. Olivia O'Leary, *Politicians and Other Animals* (Dublin: The O'Brien Press, 2004), p. 100.

3. Roddy Doyle, 'Republic Is a Beautiful Word' in *My Favourite Year: A Collection of New Football Writing*, ed. Nick Hornby (London: H., F. and G. Witherby, 1993), pp. 7-21, p. 20.

France (or Portugal) where secularists perceive the Church (*l'église*), together with the big house (*le château*), as being in alliance against the republican institutions made up of the town hall, the school and the post-office (*la mairie, l'école, et la poste*).[4] This chapter provides a brief historical overview of the political dimension of relationship between faith and culture in Ireland before exploring in detail the policy of the independent Irish State designed to reinforce the connection. I propose to look briefly at how religion and politics became intertwined at the time of the Reformation. This period is crucial in the understanding the relationship between religious and political identity in Ireland.

But, first, I wish to note that it is mistaken to conceive of Ireland as polarised simply between Gaelic/Catholic and British/Protestant. Diversity is a more pervasive and long-standing feature of Irish culture than is sometimes appreciated. Cultural diversity has been present among the inhabitants of the island long before the notion of diversity acquired its contemporary currency. To use some phrases from Louis McNeice's poem, 'Snow', our ethnic/cultural/ moral landscape is 'incorrigibly plural' and consequently 'crazier and more of it than we think'.[5]

Names to be found in Ireland today reflect wide and varied ethnic/cultural origins: Gaelic (the majority of Irish names); Norse (Harold, Sigerson, Sorensen); Norman (Norman itself, names with the prefix 'Fitz'); English (English itself, Green, Brown, Black); Scots (Scott), British (Britain); Huguenot (Blanche, Champ, D'Olier, Boucicault, Le Fanu, La Touche); Jewish (Wolfson, Goldberg, Noyek). Indeed, one of the most famous fictional characters in world literature is a Dubliner called Leopold Bloom. Then there are names such as Fleming, Holland, French and Spain that also derive from continental Europe. In bringing together, over time, people from different

4. See G. Raffi, '*Le Nouveau Combat des Laïques, Le Monde de l'Éducation, de la Culture et de la Formation*, no. 246 (mars 1997), pp. 83-84, p. 84.

5. In Kenneth Allott, *The Penguin Book of Contemporary Verse* (London: Penguin, 1968), pp. 191-2.

ethnic and cultural backgrounds in a single territory, Ireland became, in a memorable metaphor of John Hewitt's, 'a crazy knot' [6] of mixed identities.

Yet the Reformation does mark the moment around which the significant division in Irish identity assumed an explicit character. In a sense it is the crucial or defining cultural and religious hinge.

POLITICAL AND RELIGIOUS IDENTITY: AN OVERVIEW

Even in pre-Reformation Ireland we find an absence of anti-clericalism and such a vitality of religious practice as to lead commentators to note that the 'Irish are very attentive to religious matters'.[7] Another feature of Gaelic Christianity at the time, already noted in Chapter One, was 'the seamlessness of the sacred and secular spheres'.[8] This is one reason why the state-sponsored religion never took root among the general population. Another reason was educational. Lack of finance frustrated attempts by the state to establish a system of schooling that would serve to spread the doctrines of the Reformation. By contrast, many Catholic colleges in continental Europe offered education both to the clergy and also to increasing numbers of young people. This educational exchange provided the basis of 'the alternative Catholic Church'[9] that developed in the early seventeenth century. As a result, the two communities, the Old English and the Gaelic Irish, remained loyal to Catholicism. Throughout the country the recusant (Catholic) population persevered in its commitment to the traditional religious devotions and especially to the practices associated with religious guilds.

This failure to put in place the administrative machinery necessary to support educational provision was different from

6. The phrase is taken from the poem 'Ulsterman' which can be found in Patrica Craig, ed., *The Oxford Book of Ireland* (Oxford: Oxford University Press, 1999), p. 14.

7. Colm Lennon, *Sixteenth Century Ireland: The Incomplete Conquest* (Dublin: Gill and Macmillan, 1994), p. 133.

8. Ibid.

9. Ibid., p. 324.

what happened on much of the European continent where Catholic and Protestant rulers assumed for themselves the *auctoritas docendi* which had hitherto been exercised by the papacy. The Reformation rulers envisaged the authority to rule, to 'command for truth', and to educate as intimately linked. As noted in the Introduction, these rulers used their newly appropriated authority to establish an administrative infrastructure to ensure that education would promote a uniform identity that would serve to integrate their kingdoms in the cultural and religious spheres.

Another reason for the failure of the Reformation to gain adherents in the Ireland was the resistance by Gaelic Ireland to the attempts made by the English crown to promote the Protestant faith. This resistance led to an identification of Catholicism with freedom from foreign interference and this in turn prompted the development of a version of national consciousness that saw a fusing of religious, political and cultural elements. The closing years of the sixteenth century heralded the emergence of the tradition of Catholic nationhood and 'the elements of an ideology of Irish Catholic nationalism'[10] that has endured to the present. Conversely, the later Plantation of Ulster was to lead to the emergence of a version of Irishness which was eventually (particularly in the nineteenth and twentieth centuries) to associate its political identity with Britain and with Protestantism. To this day, many people associate their political and cultural sense of who they are with religion.

Awareness of the potential for social disharmony deriving from the 'crazy knot' of identities, the aspiration to separate religious from cultural and national identity formed part of the impulse behind the attempt to introduce a multi-denominational school system in the nineteenth century. The aim of the architects of the system of national education that was eventually established in Ireland in 1831 was therefore to promote a shared identity on the part of the inhabitants. The multi-denomina-

10. Ibid., p. 324.

tional system that was introduced limited the remit of the state to secular learning and assigned responsibility for religious education to the respective churches. The aim, as Lord Stanley wrote to the Duke of Leinster in 1831, was to 'unite in one system children of different creeds'.[11] The letter enjoins that the 'most scrupulous care should be taken not to interfere with the peculiar tenets of any description of Christian pupils' and invokes a report from 1812 regarding the avoidance of 'even the suspicion of proselytism'.[12] The multi-denominational project was strenuously resisted by all the Churches, with the result that education in practice assumed a denominational character.

THE EARLY YEARS

When in 1922 the Irish state was founded, a system of educational administration was already in place through which the government could realise its aim of promoting cultural nationalism and reinforce the denominational character of schooling. In the light of the salience of religion in Irish culture, this also involved the continuation and strengthening, through education, of the connection between religion and national identity.[13] Indeed, as has been noted, the Irish language, which the government undertook so eagerly to revive, gives manifold expression to this relationship.[14]

The Catholic Church, in particular, found itself dealing with a government that was sympathetic to its educational project. Three years after the foundation of the State, the Second Na-

11. These two phases are taken from the letter of Lord Stanley to the Duke of Leinster in 1831 inviting him to set up the system of National Education. The text can be found in Áine Hyland and Kenneth Milne, eds., *Irish Educational Documents*, vol. 1 (Dublin: The Church of Ireland College of Education, 1987), pp. 98-103, pp. 100-101.

12. Ibid, p. 100 and 99.

13. The use of religion in defining identity by the new State is explored in Louise Fuller, *Irish Catholicism Since 1950: The Undoing of a Culture* (Dublin: Gill and Macmillan, 2004), pp. 3-18.

14. Cultural policy with regard to the Irish language is examined in Kevin Williams, 'Reason and Rhetoric in Curriculum Policy: an appraisal of the case for the inclusion of Irish in the school curriculum', *Studies: An Irish Quarterly Review*, vol. 78, no. 310 (Summer 1989), pp. 191-203.

tional Programme Conference was held, 1925-1926. The following paragraph, which was included in the report on the conference, was adopted as policy for primary schools by the Department of Education.

Of all the parts of a school curriculum Religious Instruction is by far the most important, as its subject matter, God's honour and service, includes the proper use of all man's faculties, and affords the most powerful inducements to their proper use. We assume, therefore, that Religious Instruction is a fundamental part of the school course. Though the time allotted to it as a specific subject is necessarily short, a religious spirit should inform and vivify the whole work of the school. The teacher, — while careful, in presence of children of different religious beliefs, not to touch on matters of controversy, — should constantly inculcate, in connection with secular subjects, the practice of charity, justice, truth, purity, patience, temperance, obedience to lawful authority, and all the other moral virtues. In this way he will fulfil the primary duty of an educator, the moulding to perfect form of his pupils' character, habituating them to observe, in their relations with God and with their neighbour, the laws which God, both directly through the dictates of natural reason and through Revelation, and indirectly through the ordinance of lawful authority, imposes on mankind.[15]

Thus did the new State affirm the centrality of the religious remit of the whole primary school curriculum. This statement has constituted policy since this time, although it was not formally incorporated (in a significantly amended form) into the *Rules for National Schools* until 1965 as part of Rule 68.[16]

This was consistent with the attitude to the language. In 1922, for example, Pádraig Ó Brolcháin, the new Chief Executive

15. Áine Hyland and Kenneth Milne, eds., *Irish Educational Documents*, vol. II (Dublin: The Church of Ireland College of Education, 1992), p. 106.
16. Department of Education, *Rules for National Schools under the Department of Education* (Dublin: The Stationery Office, 1965), p. 38.

Officer for Education, argued that is should be an essential aim
of the Irish government to ensure the maintenance and 'strengthening of the national fibre by giving the language, history, music,
and tradition of Ireland their natural place in the life of Irish
schools'.[17] In 1933, in 'Notes for Teachers – Irish', the Department of Education's authors assert that it is the aim of teaching
Irish 'to ensure or preserve the cultural continuity of the nation
by putting its youth into possession of the language, literature,
history and tradition of the historic Irish people, thus fixing its
outlook in the Gaelic mould'.[18] (In the metaphors of 'fibre',
'fixing', and 'mould' clearly signalled is a sub-text of the kind of
educational endeavour envisaged.)

As William Trevor tartly puts it: 'the emergent nation, seeking
pillars on which to build itself, … plumped for holiness and the
Irish language – natural choices in the circumstances.'[19] In the
light of this policy, the criticism of Ulster poet, John Hewitt, is
hardly surprising. Although the state was 'by rebels won/ from a
torn nation', it was then 'rigged to guard their gain'.[20] And in
spite of asserting 'their love of liberty', their 'craft' then 'nar-
rowed' this 'to a fear of Rome'.[21]

The relationship between religion and cultural self-understanding comes to the fore again some fifteen years later, in 1937,
with the adoption of a new Constitution to replace the much
shorter document of 1922.[22] Even here, however, the tension
between confessional and liberal impulses in educational policy
is evident.

17. See The National Programme Conference, *Report and Programme* (Dublin,
The Stationery Office, 1926/26), p. 8, and also Hyland and Milne, eds., *Irish
Educational Documents*, Vol. II, p. 100.

18. Department of Education, 'Notes for Teachers – Irish' (Dublin: The
Stationery Office, 1933), p.1. Quoted in John Coolahan, 'Curricular Policy for
the Primary and Secondary Schools of Ireland 1900-35' (Ph. D. dissertation,
Trinity College, Dublin, 1973), p. 351.

19. William Trevor, *Beyond the Pale*, extract in Patrica Craig (ed.), *The Oxford
Book of Ireland* (Oxford: Oxford University Press, 1999), p. 424.

20. These phrases are taken from the poem 'The Dilemma' that can be found
in Patricia Craig, ed., *The Oxford Book of Ireland*, p. 300.

21. Ibid.

22. Government of Ireland, *Bunreacht na hÉireann/Constitution of Ireland*
(Dublin: The Stationery Office, 1937/1990).

THE CONSTITUTION OF 1937

As a foreign critic has noted in astonishment, the association of the nation with Christianity is very explicitly made in the Constitution, and its general tone is theocentric.[23] For example, the document is enacted and adopted 'In the name of the Most Holy Trinity, from Whom is all authority and to Whom, as our final end, all actions both of men and States must be referred, ... [while] [h]umbly acknowledging all our obligations to our Divine Lord, Jesus Christ, Who sustained our fathers through centuries of trial'. And in Article 44. 1, the 'State acknowledges that the homage of public worship is due to Almighty God. It shall hold His Name in reverence, and shall respect and honour religion'. An article giving particular prominence to the Catholic Church was also included in Article 44 of the 1937 Constitution but it was deleted following a referendum in 1972.

The State recognises the special position of the Holy Catholic Apostolic and Roman Church as the guardian of the Faith professed by the majority of the citizens.

However, another provision, that was also deleted in the same referendum, referred to the role of other religious traditions in Irish life.

The State also recognises the Church of Ireland, the Presbyterian Church in Ireland, the Methodist Church in Ireland, the Religious Society of Friends in Ireland, as well as the Jewish Congregations and the other religious denominations existing in Ireland at the date of the coming into operation of this Constitution.

The liberal impulse is further reflected in the following clauses that also appear in Article 44 and which are still in force.

2.1 Freedom of conscience and the free profession and practice of religion are, subject to public order and morality,

23. Régis Debray, *L'Enseignement du Fait Religieux dans L'École Laïque* (Paris: Editions Odile Jacob, 2002), pp. 44-5.

guaranteed to every citizen.

2.2 The State guarantees not to endow any religion.

2.3 The State shall not impose any disabilities or make any discrimination on the ground of religious profession, belief or status.

Moreover, in the provisions relevant to education, the Constitution confers upon the State no direct role in the religious formation of citizens. In Article 42, which deals with education, an undertaking is given that the 'State shall ... as guardian of the common good, require in view of actual conditions that the children receive a certain minimum education, moral, intellectual and social' (42. 3. 2) but the article offers no undertaking in respect of a minimum religious education. Responsibility is assigned to parents 'to provide, according to their means, for the religious and moral, intellectual, physical and social education of their children' (Art. 42. 1). To this end, the 'State shall not oblige parents in violation of their conscience and lawful preference to send their children to schools established by the State, or to any particular type of school designated by the State' (Art. 42. 3. 1).

Those who drafted this guarantee could hardly have envisaged how it would be invoked against denominational schooling. This neatly illustrates one of the lessons of history in Church-State relations, namely, that laws can have unpredictable consequences.[24]

Nevertheless, in its support of education, the State must show 'due regard ... for the rights of parents, especially in the matter of religious and moral formation' (Art. 42. 4). This regard is reinforced by the provision in Article 44 (which deals with religion). It states:

Legislation providing State aid for schools shall not discriminate between schools under the management of different religious denominations, nor be such as to affect prejudicially

---

24. See Harry Judge, *Faith-based Schools and the State: Catholics in America, France and England* (Oxford: Symposium Book, 2002), pp. 258-263.

the right of any child to attend a school receiving public money without receiving religious instruction at that school (Art. 44. 2. 4).

The guarantees in the Constitution regarding the right to withdraw from religious education reflect the historical provisions made in respect of primary schools that were to be repeated later in respect of Vocational Schools/Community Colleges and Community Schools. In these schools parents have the right 'to request in writing that their children be withdrawn from classes in religious instruction'.[25] In Community Schools, religious instruction and religious worship are provided 'except for such pupils whose parents make a request in writing to the Principal that those pupils should be withdrawn from religious worship or religious instruction or both religious worship and religious instruction'.[26]

In spite of the constitutional right to withdraw from religious education, the rules of the Department of Education for vocational schools, which are under the control of local authorities, endorse a view of religion as an integral part of the cultural identity to be promoted in these schools. This system of state/ local authority Vocational/Technical Schools was established in 1930, although the document (*Memorandum V. 40*) laying down the principles underlying the schools was not published until 1942. Let us examine these rules more closely.

VOCATIONAL EDUCATION

There was much discussion between the Minister and the Catholic hierarchy about the character of vocational schools and the content of their curriculum. The animating principles of vocational (called continuation) education were certainly designed to be acceptable to the Church. Very strong affirmations, which are still in force, are made about the relationship between

25. Department of Education, Circular letter No. 7/79: Religious Instruction in Vocational Schools (Dublin: Department of Education, 1979).
26. Association of Community Schools, Model Lease for Community Schools (Dublin; Association of Community Schools, 1992), p. 23.

religion and the development of national identity. The Introduction to *Memorandum V. 40*, published in 1942, states that all schools which provide continuation education must ensure that such education 'be in keeping with Irish tradition and should reflect in the schools the loyalty to our Divine Lord which is expressed in the Prologue and Articles of the Constitution'.[27] It then proposes the 'integration' of religion with national culture as 'a task calling for the co-operative efforts of all teachers' in order to provide within the school a 'unity' which would reflect that of the 'good home' which is described as 'the model for ordered social life' where 'tradition, faith, work and recreation blend naturally and easily with one another'.[28]

The conception of education underlying the document is unambiguously Christian. The Introduction affirms that the 'general purpose of continuation education is to help each pupil to secure his own ultimate good'.[29] Later in the document, in the section entitled 'General Organisation of Continuation Courses', elaboration is provided regarding this purpose and the character of this 'ultimate good'. The 'general purpose' of continuation education is:

> to develop, with the assistance of God's grace, the whole man with all his faculties, natural and supernatural, so that he may realise his duties and responsibilities as a member of society, that he may contribute effectively to the welfare of his fellow man, and by so doing attain the end designed for him by his Creator.[30]

In the body of the document, following reference to the appointment of teachers of religion, under the heading 'Reli-

27. Department of Education, *Memorandum V. 40; Organisation of Whole-time Continuation Courses in Borough, Urban and County Areas, 1942* (Dublin: Department of Education, 1942). The quotations from this document (except the last one) can be found in Hyland and Milne, *Irish Educational Documents*, vol. II, pp. 224-232, p. 225.
28. Ibid, p. 226.
29. Ibid.
30. Ibid., p. 230.

gious Instruction and Social Education', it is stated that 'every
effort should be made to collaborate with [teachers of religion]
in their work'.[31] The document then continues:

> This collaboration is essential to the production of really
> fruitful results from vocational education. It is necessary not
> only that religious instruction be given at certain times, but
> also that the teaching of every other subject be permeated
> with Christian charity, and that the whole organisation of the
> school, whether in work or recreation be regulated by the
> same spirit. In the nature of the case all teachers have oppor-
> tunities each day of showing the practical applications of
> religious doctrine, and can do much to form the characters of
> their pupils by inspiring them to acts of supernatural virtue
> and self-sacrifice.[32]

The document then goes on to state that '[s]ocial education
is closely associated with religious instruction' in 'the right
formation of citizens'[33] – a conjunction of religious with civic/
social formation which is also pronounced in later documents.

LATER DOCUMENTS
Before examining the relationship between religious and
civic education, the general thrust of policy with regard to
primary education must be considered. Although the focus of
this volume is on documents that form actual state policy, it is
worth noting that *The Report of the Council of Education on the
Function and the Curriculum of the Primary School, 1954* endorsed
very emphatically the denominational and catechetical character of primary education.[34] The spirit of this document informs

31. Ibid., p. 231.
32. Ibid.
33. In Memorandum V. 40 only.
34. See Hyland and Milne, *Irish Educational Documents*, vol. II, pp. 119-125.
There is an interesting discussion of this document and of the *Report of the Council
of Education on the Curriculum of the Secondary School, 1962* in Louise Fuller, *Irish
Catholicism Since 1950: The Undoing of a Culture* (Dublin: Gill and Macmillan,
2004), pp. 11-12.

very strongly the treatment of the role of religion from 1965 to1971. Let us dwell a little on this spirit as it captures very dramatically the mindset of the times. Paragraph 194 opens with the confident proclamation that in

> Ireland, happily, there is no disagreement as to the place religion should occupy in the school. Through many centuries our people have striven to secure the freedom to have children taught in schools conducted in accordance with the parents' religious concept of life.[35]

The authors' description of parents' values is striking. The document attributes to them the view that religion

> was not merely one of many subjects to be taught in the school: it was the soul, the foundation and the crown of the whole educational process, giving value and meaning to every subject in the curriculum.[36]

The language condemning the 1831 system of multi-denominational schooling is uncompromising. The 'undenominational principle underlying' this system is characterised as 'obnoxious to our people'.[37] In Paragraph 195, the authors assert that not only are the National schools of the time 'essentially religious and denominational in character' but also that 'their primary purpose is religious'.[38]

PRIMARY EDUCATION

In 1965, an edited version of the long statement, previously quoted, which emanated from the Second National Programme Conference of 1925-26, was formally incorporated into the *Rules for National Schools*. In the amended document, the admonition to be 'careful, in presence of children of different religious

---

35. Ibid., p. 124.
36. Ibid.
37. Ibid.
38. Ibid.

beliefs, not to touch on matters of controversy', was deleted.[39] Requirements regarding the timetabling of Religious Instruction were made less stringent one result being that it became more difficult to withdraw children from these lessons.[40] No longer was it necessary to schedule Religious Instruction at the beginning or end of the school day, although the hours of such instruction still had to be fixed.[41]

This document followed the recommendation of *The Report of the Council of Education on the Function and the Curriculum of the Primary School, 1954* that the 'fullness of denominational education ... be legally sanctioned' [42] and accordingly gave 'explicit recognition to the denominational character'[43] of state-sponsored primary schools. In the light of this affirmation of the 'denominational character' of schools, it was probably felt that the precautions were no longer necessary. As we shall see in the next chapter, the Green Paper of 1992 was to describe these moves as 'weakening the protections that existed for children of religious beliefs different to those of the majority in the schools'.[44]

When in 1971 a new curriculum for primary schools was introduced, the statement from the Second National Programme Conference in the *Rules for National Schools* was repeated in *The Primary School Curriculum: Teachers' Handbook* together with the following commentary. 'It is felt that this statement needs no further elaboration as a declaration of the principles by which

39. Department of Education, *Rules for National Schools under the Department of Education* (Dublin: The Stationery Office, 1965), p. 38. See also Hyland. and Milne, *Irish Educational Documents*, vol. II, p. 135. We should note, however, that this admonition is to be found in the 1946 version of Department of Education, *Rules for National Schools under the Department of Education* (Dublin: The Stationery Office, 1946), p. 43. This document says 'in the presence' rather than 'in presence'.

40. See Hyland and Milne, *Irish Educational Documents*, Vol. II, p. 135.

41. Ibid.

42. Ibid., p. 125.

43. Department of Education, *Rules for National Schools under the Department of Education*, 1965, p. 8. See also Hyland and Milne, *Irish Educational Documents*, vol II, p. 135.

44. Government of Ireland, *Education for A Changing World: Green Paper on Education* (Dublin: The Stationery Office, 1992), p. 90

Religious Instruction in our primary schools is animated.'[45] The statement is consistent with the section 'Primary Education: Aims and Function'. Here we read:

> Each human being is created in God's image. He has a life to lead and a soul to be saved. Education is, therefore, concerned not only with life but with the purpose of life. And, since all men are equal in the eyes of God, each is entitled to an equal chance of obtaining optimum personal fulfilment.[46]

The Primary School Curriculum: Teacher's Handbook advocates very strongly the principles of the integrated curriculum; so it is hardly surprising to find that the document attributes a crucial role to religious education in promoting this integration.

> [T]he separation of religious and secular instruction into differentiated subject compartments serves only to throw the whole educational function out of focus ... The integration of the curriculum may be seen:-
>   (i) in the religious and civic spirit which animates all its parts.[47]

Every subject is envisaged as helping 'the child to achieve a proper relationship with God, with his neighbour and with his environment'.[48] One of the principal purposes of Social and Environmental Studies is to develop in children 'an appreciation of Nature as the work of God.'[49]

The statement that there is a very close relationship between religious formation and education for citizenship is striking, and it merits some attention as it is particularly germane to the theme of faith and nationhood.

45. Department of Education, *Curraclam na Bunscoile: Lámhleabhar an Oide/ Primary School Curriculum: Teacher's Handbook* : *Parts One and Two* (Dublin: The Stationery Office, 1971), Part One, p. 23.
    46. Ibid., p. 12.
    47. Ibid., p. 19.
    48. Department of Education, *Curraclam na Bunscoile: Lámhleabhar an Oide/ Primary School Curriculum: Teacher's Handbook: Parts One and Two*, Part Two, p. 117
    49. Ibid., p. 12.

RELIGION AND CIVIC EDUCATION

As was pointed out in the section on vocational education, in the 'right formation of citizens', social education was conceived as 'closely associated' with religion. In introducing the subject 'Civics' at second level in 1966, the authors of the Department of Education's document argue that religious education is primary and that moral education and, by extension, civic education, derive from religious principles. 'During his religious studies especially', they write:

the pupil will have instilled into him the virtues of charity, honesty, self-sacrifice, purity and temperance and will acquire a complete moral code which will serve as the chief guide of his conduct and the mainspring of his actions and thinking.[50]

It is noted that civics is not

to be regarded as a substitute for religious and moral training nor for that training in character formation and general behaviour which is an essential objective of all education, but rather, again, as the complement to and extension of such training. Its concern will be the imbuing of the pupil with the social and civic principles which help in the formation of the good citizen.[51]

The dependence of civic education upon religion is also evident in the 'Notes on the Teaching of Civics' published in the same year.

It is not difficult to see the importance of co-ordinating civics with religious instruction ... It would not be very effective for the civics teacher to discuss with his pupils the political and social duties of the citizen unless the moral principles underlying those duties had already been dealt with in the religious instruction class.[52]

50. Department of Education, *Rules and Programme for Secondary Schools* (Dublin: The Stationery Office, 1966 in 1986/1987 edition), p. 165.
51. Ibid.
52. Department of Education, 'Notes on the Teaching of Civics' (Dublin: Department of Education, 1966). p. 3.

The following is a proposed sample treatment of a section of the prescribed syllabus dealing with 'Religion and the State: the provisions of the Constitution regarding religion. The various denominations'.[53] This will involve study of

> Religion and the individual's ultimate destiny; its importance to the family, to society in general, to the nation, to the international community of nations; rights and duties; the reasons for and the importance of religious toleration; respect for denominations other than one's own [;] a brief study of denominations represented locally.
>
> A brief study of the relevant sections of the Constitution in the light of what has been discussed above.[54]

The conceptual link between civic and religious education is not as pronounced in the 1971 curriculum for primary schools. On the one hand, both areas are seen to 'share much common ground in the knowledge they seek to impart and the attitudes and virtues they aim to develop' and as a result '[t]here is obviously a very close affinity between Religious Education and Civics'.[55] But the authors go on to reject the 'narrow viewpoint that matters of morals and behaviour belong exclusively to the sphere of the churches' and affirm the importance of encouraging pupils to 'embrace' moral values 'by personal choice' in the light of 'an upright conscience'.[56] Nonetheless, the religious dimension of civic education is articulated clearly. For instance, it is suggested that in the study of the family 'the love of Christ for His mother, His life as a member of the Holy Family and other aspects of the Divine example might be presented to the children as the ideal'.[57] The form of patriotism recommended must '[a]bove all ... prove itself in its consistency with duty to God and to the moral law'.[58]

53. Ibid., p. 4.
54. Ibid., p. 5.
55. Department of Education, *Curraclam na Bunscoile: Lámhleabhar an Oide/ Primary School Curriculum: Teacher's Handbook: Parts One and Two*, Part Two, p. 116.
56. Ibid.
57. Ibid., p. 122.
58. Ibid., p. 124.

CONCLUSION

From tthe texts presented in his chapter it is clear, as Declan Kiberd puts it with characteristic eloquence and insight, that the Catholic ethos

which had pervaded schools for two centuries had never been clearly defined, largely because it was assumed to be unproblematic and all-pervasive. What was to take its place was not at all obvious.[59]

Yet the status of religion was to change as the place of religion in general educational policy became a matter of direct concern in the Green and White Papers of the 1990s. This was due to an increasingly pluralist spirit in the country and to challenges to the hegemony of the ideology of Catholic nationalism.

59. D. Kiberd, *Inventing Ireland: The Literature of the Modern Nation* (London: Vintage, 1996), p. 573.

CHAPTER THREE

Responding to
the Liberal Challenge

This chapter considers the challenge to government policy regarding the role of religion in education on the grounds that it infringed the civil liberties of non-religious citizens or of citizens who did not share the Christian ethos of the school. The challenge was to the catechetical character of Religious Education at primary and second level and, particularly, to the policy and practice of integrating religion and the general curriculum at primary level.

Before embarking on a more detailed study of the subject, let me clarify some matters. Firstly, for the sake of convenience I shall normally refer to the children of non-believing or non-religious parents although the children may not share the views or the wishes of their parents. Secondly, not all non-religious parents object to schools with a confessional ethos; and, thirdly, the enrolment of so many Catholic children in Educate Together schools indicates that many Catholic parents prefer non-confessional schools.

To understand the liberal challenge, it might help to provide a brief overview of the school situation in Ireland.

RELIGION IN IRISH SCHOOLS

At primary level schools are largely state-aided, with the state providing the major proportion of capital and current expenditure in order to supplement the educational initiatives of denominational and other bodies. Excluding some 125 schools for children with special educational needs, in 2002/3 there were some 3,154 state-supported primary schools – 2,919 were under the control of the Catholic Church. The remainder divided along the following lines: 198 schools were under the control of various Protestant denominations, 30 were multi-denominational, one was Jewish and two were Muslim.[1]

At second level, the State provides much of the finance to support schools (416) owned largely by religious bodies. Almost one third of second level schools (247) (known as Vocational Schools and more recently Community Colleges) are, however, directly state-owned and are funded through local authorities. From the late 1960s, a new model of second-level school, known originally as Comprehensive Schools and subsequently as Community Schools, has emerged. There are some 87 of these schools and they combine, through a deed of trust, a management partnership of state/local authority and denominational interests. They also provide a model for school amalgamations and are the model of second-level schooling likely to be favoured in the future.[2]

At primary level, one half-hour per day is devoted to what is called 'religious instruction' (see below). This is provided under the guidance of the relevant religious authorities and the State has no role apart from ensuring that no child is obliged to attend religion class against the wishes of his/her parents. Normally the regular class teacher also takes the daily lesson in Religious Education and teachers in denominational primary schools are indeed expected to do so. However, where a teacher objects on grounds of conscience, then in practice arrangements may be made for that teacher to undertake other duties while someone else takes the class in religion.

At secondary level, teachers of religion are paid the normal incremental salary by the State to provide two hours teaching of religion to each class per week. In state schools their appointment must be approved by the 'catechetical inspectorate' and

1. These statistics were compiled by the INTO and can be found in Irish National Teachers' Organisation, *Teaching Religion in the Primary School: Issues and Challenges* (Dublin: Irish National Teachers' Organisation, 2003), Appendix One, p. 143.

2. These are the figures for 2001/2 taken from the website of the Department of Education and Science (www.education.ie), from the section on Statistics, Key Statistics about the Department's Customers. Accessed 25 March 2004.

provision can be made to transfer teachers of religion to other duties if they cease to be acceptable to the relevant religious authorities.[3] Until the introduction of Religious Education as an examination subject made possible by the Education Act in 1998, the curriculum in Religious Education was solely within the control of the relevant denominational authorities.

The arrangements for Religious Education in Educate Together schools are very different. Autumn 2004 saw the publication of the sector's common programme in moral, civic, spiritual and Religious Education. Entitled *Learn Together: An Ethical Education Curriculum for Educate Together Schools*, it is compulsory for all pupils. In this programme, pupils are taught about worldviews with the aim of fostering tolerance and respect for different traditions in the context of promoting an agreed set of moral principles. Provision for denominationally-specific religious instruction for those pupils whose parents seek it, is made outside schools hours. (In Chapter Six there is discussion of the approach taken in Educate Together schools.)

An interdominational model has been developed within the context of *Scoileanna Lán Ghaeilge* under the auspices of *Foras Patrúnachta Scoileanna Lán Ghaeilge*. This involves a joint Catholic and Protestant inter-denominational religious programme. The teaching of religion is conducted on an ecumenical basis to all pupils in the same classroom during school hours. Protestant children may either be offered special instruction during the time allocated for preparation for the Catholic sacraments or may remain as part of the class. As interdenominational schools are so new, much of the fine detail is being worked out on the ground.[4]

3. Department of Education, Circular letter No. 7/79: Religious Instruction in Vocational Schools (Dublin: Department of Education, 1979). See also Association of Community Schools, Model Lease for Community Schools (Dublin: Association of Community Schools, 1992).

4. The issue is discussed by Pádraig Hogan in 'Religion in Education and the Integrity of Teaching as a Practice: The Experience of Irish National Schools in Changing Times' in *Teaching Religion in the Primary School: Issues and Challenges*, Irish National Teachers' Organisation, (Dublin: Irish National Teachers' Organisation, 2003), pp. 69-71.

The Catechetical Character of Religious Education

The teaching of religion in the overwhelming majority of schools was therefore catechetical in character at both primary and second level. This meant that it had as its purpose the continued initiation of young people into the faith and the consolidation of their commitment to it.

The first aspect of the liberal challenge to state policy was to the catechetical character of the teaching of religion. As noted above, the profile of Religious Education at second level changed with its introduction as an examination subject. (This theme will be developed in the next chapter.) In any case, it was the 0primary level that was of most concern to policy-makers. Although parents had the right to withdraw their children from religion class, it was not always possible for schools, for practical reasons regarding space and personnel, to make alternative arrangements to accommodate children withdrawn from Religious Education. Even where parents did ask to have their children withdrawn, this withdrawal could be said to have had a stigmatising effect leaving the children vulnerable to teasing and bullying.[5]

Withdrawal was even more complicated in the years when children were being prepared for Communion and Confirmation as activities related to this preparation often required a more extensive time allocation than the normal half-hour per day.

The Integrated Curriculum and the Right to Withdraw
from Religious Education

This takes us to the second aspect of the challenge. As we have seen, parents enjoyed the constitutional right to withdraw their children from Religious Education in the formative sense but it was hard to see how such withdrawal could be complete or absolute in practice. This was because the rules of the Department of Education required the maintenance of a religious ethos in all primary schools. This requirement was part of Rule 68 of

5. See David Alvey, *Irish Education: The Case for Secular Reform* (Dublin and Belfast: Church and State Books/Athol Books, 1991), Part One.

the *Rules for National Schools* promulgated in 1965 ('a religious spirit should inform and vivify the whole work of the school'). The other strand of the requirement was via the mandatory relationship between religion and other subjects through the integrated curriculum in the *Primary School Curriculum* of 1971.

A similar integrative role is attributed to religion in the regulations that govern the operation of VEC schools at second level but this never became problematic.

These affirmations of the place of religion as the integrating principle of the whole curriculum made it very hard to see how withdrawal from indirect religious instruction could be realised in practice. Note that these were requirements of the State rather than of the Churches. The charge was made that school authorities were infringing the rights of non-believers and imposing a theistic worldview on children whose parents objected to this worldview.

In order to understand the context in which the issue arises, it is necessary briefly to sketch some relevant background in educational thought.

Integration within the Curriculum

Before dealing with the role of religion in curriculum integration, let us consider the notion of integration itself. Integration means that, wherever relevant or appropriate, the necessary connections between different areas of the school curriculum are not only acknowledged but also emphasised and promoted. Indeed long before fashionable advocacy of curriculum integration and the condemnation of subject 'compartmentalisation' in the 1960s and 1970s, good teachers have practised curricular integration.

Integration is often either a feature of, or a possibility within, much of the school curriculum. For example, it is impossible fully to understand certain works of art without studying some history just as the serious study of some historical periods can require the study of the art of the time. The study of some of Yeats's poems requires understanding of the historical context in which they were written and the study of the Renaissance requires study of its art. Another illustration of this practice would be where the study of ecological issues in geography leads to the study of the nature poetry. Similarly, the teaching of a foreign language might be set in a context that encourages study of the historical, political and geographical aspects of the country where the language is spoken. In this perspective, it is hardy surprising that 88% of teacher respondents to a 1996 INTO survey stated that they taught 'aspects of the curriculum on an integrated basis'.[6]

As religion provides a way of apprehending the world that informs the whole life of believers and provides the spring of moral commitments to act in ways which are consistent with realising their ultimate destiny, it is not surprising that religion offers considerable scope for curricular integration. Religious themes directly arise in the arts, and consideration of the influence of religion on human affairs arises in the study of history. Religion offers answers to the great metaphysical questions regarding creation and about humankind's nature and purpose that can arise in teaching science or geography. Religious beliefs inform views about human moral responsibility that arise in teaching literature and about human sexuality that arise in teaching biology and home economics. Moral issues arise as well in such subjects as business studies or technology.

In view of the integrative role attributed to religion in Vocational Schools, we should note that the teaching of practical subjects can in fact be invested with a religious dimension. This derives from the Christian understanding of human action as participation in the creative activity of God – an understanding that is rooted in the great monastic, notably Benedictine, tradition of Christendom whose monasteries have always been places of labour as well as of learning. Where the teaching of practical subjects is animated by such a view, this teaching involves *pari*

6. Irish National Teachers' Organisation, *Primary School Curriculum: an Evolutionary Process* (Dublin: INTO, 1996), p. 46.

passu communicating an aspect of the religious response to the world. In brief, some level of integration between school subjects is inevitable as well as desirable.

The relationship between cultural initiation and religious faith is commonly given expression in the school curriculum in Ireland. We can look, for example, at the vision of creation held by country teacher and distinguished writer, Bryan MacMahon. Writing of how he envisages textbooks in Religious Education, MacMahon urges that they should 'obliquely – and poetically, if at all possible – stress or convey, even by implication, the knowledge of God as shown in his creation'.[7]

He then goes on to evoke in his inimitably poetic fashion the action of God in the wonderful detail and variety of creation. This is exhibited in the complex and subtle order of the universe expressed in the rhythm of the seasons, the life-cycles of vegetable, insects, fish and other creatures and in the whole teeming world of nature as well as in 'the cunning and delectable fashion in which man and woman mortise and tenon to form new human beings'.[8]

MacMahon then asks whether it is possible to conceive of this as other than the action of God. MacMahon's approach reminds me of Einstein's description of himself as like a 'religious worshipper or lover' absorbing the 'silence of the high mountains where the eye ranges freely through the still pure air and fondly traces out the restful contours apparently built for eternity ... ' [9]

MacMahon's conception of the origin and purposes of human life would lead to the promotion of a theological world view about creation and humankind's nature and purpose in teaching science, geography, environmental studies and would lead also to the conduct of sexuality education in theological terms. This perspective would be shared by many teachers in Irish schools and is bound to influence teaching across the whole

7. Bryan MacMahon, *The Master* (Dublin: Poolbeg, 1992), p. 105.
8. Ibid.
9. Quoted in P. D. Walsh, *Education and Meaning: Philosophy in Practice* (London: Cassell, 1993), p. 103.

curriculum and it is hardly surprising to find that the INTO research just mentioned confirms the presence of substantial integration between religion and other areas of the curriculum at primary level.[10]

The Irish Dimension

The presence of integration between religion and other school subjects is quite explicit throughout the Irish school curriculum at primary and second levels. This is hardly surprising in the light of the general profile of religion in Irish culture as elaborated in Chapter One. To this day, many people's political and cultural sense of who they are is associated with religion. Civic education and the more formal study of history in Irish schools are therefore bound to concern themselves with these dimensions of cultural self-understanding. This is not to claim that the religious aspects of the different versions of Irish identity must be reinforced (as traditionally they have been) but they must be taken into account. Cultural and political identity must be defined in relation to the religious traditions of the island. Given how inextricably linked are religion and culture in Irish life, the findings of the INTO research regarding the presence of substantial integration between religion and other areas of the curriculum make perfect sense.[11]

And it is the explicit practice of such integration which has become a cause of concern to policy-makers. Examples would include the promotion of a theological worldview about creation and humankind's nature and purpose in teaching science, geography, environmental studies, or the conduct of sexuality education in terms of specifically Christian moral principles. But it is in the teaching of English and Irish where the integration of the sacred and the secular is perhaps most readily identifiable.

Here we should note a distinction to be made between teaching literature that simply deals with religious themes and

10. Irish National Teachers' Organisation, *Primary School Curriculum: an Evolutionary Process*, p. 46.
11. Ibid.

teaching it in a way that could be said to reinforce the Christian worldview. The teaching of poems with religious themes was not the issue for opponents of the role of religion in the integrated curriculum. Rather it was the presence in primary school readers in Irish and English of literature that reinforced the Christian worldview. An example would be treating the lines by Joyce Kilmer – 'I think that I shall never see/A poem lovely as a tree. / Poems are made by fools like me/But only God can make a tree' – as if they expressed an incontrovertible truth about the world. Some of the material used in Irish primary readers was quite explicit in its promotion of a theological view of the world. For instance, a poem in a sixth class reader, *The Crock of Gold*, entitled 'All Around' by Leonard Clark, contained three stanzas each one developing the thought in its first line – 'We can see Him all around/We can hear Him all around/We can find Him all around'.[12] A reader in Irish, *An Scealaí*, contained a similar poem called '*Dia a chum gach aon rud*' and the last page of this text contained an eight line poem entitled *'Paidir'*.[13] Another series (*Let's Go*) made use of the account of the Christmas narrative from St Luke's gospel as well as Chesterton's poem 'The Donkey' which deals with the part played by the donkey in Christ's entry into Jerusalem on Palm Sunday.[14]

THE GOVERNMENT'S RESPONSE

The place of religion in general educational policy, especially in respect of the integrated curriculum, became a matter of direct concern in the Green and White Papers of the 1990s. As we have seen, the status of Religious Education in schools in Ireland is complex and its treatment in the government documents of

12. C.J. Fallon, *The Crock of Gold* (Stage 4, book 2, Rainbow Reading Programme, (Dublin: Fallons, 1984).

13. An Comhlucht Oideachais , *An Scealaí,* Céime 3, Leabhar B, Duilleoga, (Baile Atha Cliath: An Comhlucht Oideachais, 1989).

14. Roberta Reener-Tauch/John Killeen, *Let's Go:* Stage 4, Book 2 (Dublin: Gill and Macmillan, 1983). On this theme see James Bennett, 'Changing values in primary education', *Studies: An Irish Quarterly Review,* vol. 84, no. 333 (1995), pp. 71-79.

the 1990s, principally the Green Paper on education of 1992 and in the White Paper of 1995, reflects this complexity.

Religion and Religious Education

The tone of the Green Paper in its treatment of religion is very different from that of previous documents such as *The Primary Teacher's Handbook* and *The Rules for National School*. Where matters of religion and spirituality are mentioned, they are treated in a dispassionate tone as aspects of a culture which merit being critically understood rather than assimilated in any formative sense. In this perspective we read of '[f]ostering an understanding and critical appreciation of the values – moral, spiritual, social and cultural – of the home and society generally' and of aiming to 'develop' in young people 'an understanding of their own religious beliefs and a tolerance for the beliefs of others'.[15] Consistent with this emphasis is a tendency to interpret Religious Education narrowly in terms of instruction in a religious faith. This means that the implications of belief for general values education and for the full personal development of young people are overlooked.

By contrast, the tone of the White Paper with regard to Religious Education is more balanced, nuanced and sensitive than that of the Green Paper. Whereas the Green Paper refers to the aim of '[f]ostering an understanding and critical appreciation of the values – moral, spiritual, social and cultural – of the home and society generally', the White Paper speaks of fostering an 'understanding and critical appreciation of the values – moral, spiritual, religious, social and cultural – which have been distinctive in shaping Irish society and which have been traditionally accorded respect in society'.[16] The change in tone is also marked in the treatment of the role of Religious Education at junior cycle of secondary school. The Green Paper states that '[r]eligious education should form part of the available pro-

---

15. Government of Ireland, *Education for A Changing World: Green Paper on Education* (Dublin: The Stationery Office, 1992), pp. 33 and 87.
16. *Education for A Changing World: Green Paper on Education*, p. 33, *Charting Our Education Future: White Paper on Education*, p. 10.

gramme for all students, with due regard to the constitutional rights of parents related to the participation of their children'.[17]

The objective of the White Paper, on the other hand, is that by the end of junior cycle/compulsory schooling 'all students, in accordance with their abilities and aptitudes', will have enjoyed 'formative experiences in moral, religious and spiritual education'.[18] Religious Education is included as one of the areas which '[e]ach school will be expected to provide'[19] and no reference is made to the right of parents to withdraw their children from Religious Education. No doubt this right is assumed but the authors of the White Paper reasonably felt that it was unnecessary to labour the obvious.

Although the White Paper does not refer to the status of religion at senior cycle, this is consistent with the treatment of the standard curriculum for the Leaving Certificate where the role of individual subjects is not explored. Yet, in so far as provision 'at senior cycle will be characterised by continuity with and progression from junior cycle'[20], there could be said to be an implied recognition of the place of Religious Education at this level.

The Right to Withdraw from Religious Education

Although already enshrined in the Constitution and endorsed in Department of Education documents, the right of non-believing parents to withdraw their children from Religious Education is a preoccupation in both documents, although as noted above, the issue is less laboured in the White Paper. In the section of the Green Paper dealing with Religious Education in the primary school, it is asserted explicitly and forcefully several times. Concern is expressed that

> changes made to the *Rules for National Schools* over time, and embodied in the *Rules* published in 1965, could be seen to

---

17. *Education for A Changing World: Green Paper on Education*, p. 96.
18. *Charting Our Education Future: White Paper on Education*, pp. 46-7.
19. Ibid., p. 48.
20. Ibid., p. 52.

have the effect of weakening the protections that existed for children of religious beliefs different to those of the majority in the schools.[21]

Here the authors are referring to the changes mentioned in Chapter Two, especially to the requirement of teachers to be 'careful, in presence of children of different religious beliefs, not to touch on issues of controversy' which was removed from Rule 68 in the edition of *Rules for National Schools* published in 1965. The passage then continues:

> The general review of the *Rules for National Schools*, recommended by the Primary Education Review body, will seek also to ensure that all aspects of the *Rules* fully reflect the relevant articles of the Constitution. Furthermore, the 1971 *Teachers' Handbook for the Primary School*, as part of its promotion of an integrated curriculum, also sought to integrate religious and secular instruction. The *Handbook* will be reviewed to ensure that the constitutional rights of children are fully safeguarded.[22]

But what is not stated is whether the changes envisaged would simply involve the removal of the reference to the centrality of religion in the primary curriculum and of the requirement that religion serve as a important element in curriculum integration or whether overt reference to religion would be prohibited outside the time set aside for religious instruction.

The rights of non-believing parents were also considered in the *Report on the National Education Convention* that notes, for example, that where parents withdraw their children from religion class, this may have 'peer-stigmatising effects'.[23] The general thrust of the treatment of the issue in the *Report on the National Education Convention* is reflected in the White Paper. The White Paper reaffirms '**the right of schools in accordance with their**

21. *Education for A Changing World: Green Paper on Education*, p. 90.
22. Ibid., pp. 90/91.
23. The Convention Secretariat, John Coolahan (ed.), *Report on the National Education Convention* (Dublin: The Stationery Office, 1993), p. 33.

religious ethos, to provide denominational religious education and instruction to their students, while underpinning the constitutional rights of parents to withdraw their children from religious education instruction.'[24] (bold type in original)

The document also re-affirms the commitment to '**ensure that the Constitutional rights of children are fully safeguarded**' (bold type in original) and to review the *Rules for National Schools* and *Teachers' Handbook* in revising the primary curriculum.[25] In this perspective, the Department of Education, 'while recognising and supporting the denominational ethos of schools', will require that all schools 'ensure that the rights of those who do not subscribe to the school's ethos are protected in a caring manner'.[26] The document shows particular concern that a balance be struck between the

> rights, obligations and choices of the majority of parents and students, who subscribe to the ethos of a school, and those in a minority, who may not subscribe to that ethos, but who do not have the option, for practical reasons, to select a school which reflects their particular choices.[27]

The issue is raised again in the final chapter of the document that examines the legal and constitutional framework for education. It is argued that the denominational character of schools

> must be reasonable and proportionate to the legitimate aim of preserving the ethos of schools and must balance this right of schools and their students against the rights to education of students of different denominations or none and the rights of teachers to earn a livelihood.[28]

The rights of teachers and, in particular the relationship between private lifestyle and professional role featured in the

---

24. Government of Ireland, *Charting Our Education Future: White Paper on Education*, p. 23.
25. Ibid.
26. Ibid.
27. Ibid., pp. 23/24.
28. Ibid., p. 217

widely publicised court case concerning Eileen Flynn who was dismissed from her teaching post in a voluntary secondary school on grounds of a lifestyle inconsistent with the ethos of the school. The dismissal was upheld in a decision of the High Court.[29]

To address all of these matters, the Convention Report proposes that a working party be established to develop the 'good practice' guidelines recommended by the *Report on the National Education Convention*.[30] Regrettably, this committee has not been established.

The attempt to reconcile the claims of religious and secular versions of human self-understanding in modern Ireland, nevertheless, remained an important feature of educational policy in the late 1990s. Educational policy was one aspect of a general attempt to determine the relationship between Church and State in contemporary Ireland. The two pillars of State policy were to remove from the State any role in prescribing the character of the ethos of schools on a national basis and to confer on individual schools discretion with regard to the ethos that they wished to embrace.

THE EDUCATION ACT

This policy is reflected in the State's first Education Act. On the one hand, the State will endeavour to ensure that the education system 'in the interests of the common good ... respects the diversity of values, beliefs, languages and traditions in Irish society'.[31] On the other hand a 'recognised school shall ... promote the moral, spiritual, social and personal development of students and provide health education for them, in consultation with their parents, having regard to the characteristic spirit of the school'.[32] This spirit, which the Board of

29. See *Eileen Flynn v Sister Anna Power and the Sisters of the Holy Faith*: High Court (Circuit Court Appeal) (Costello J.) 8 March 1985, *Irish Law Review Monthly* (1985), pp. 336-343.

30. Government of Ireland, *Charting Our Education Future: White Paper on Education*, p. 23.

31. Government of Ireland, *Education Act 1998* (Dublin: The Stationery Office), Preamble.

32. Ibid., Section 9 (d).

Management shall 'uphold, and be accountable to the patron for so upholding' is 'determined by the cultural, educational, moral, religious, social, linguistic and spiritual values and traditions which inform and are characteristic of the objectives and conduct of the school'.[33]

The Act also imposes on the Minister for Education an obligation to 'have regard to the characteristic spirit of a school or class of school in exercising his or her functions'.[34]

The Education Act also has the 'following objects': 'to give practical effect to the constitutional rights of children'[35] and 'to promote the right of parents to send their children to a school of the parents' choice having regard to the rights of patrons and the effective and efficient use of resources'.[36] A 'recognised school' is also obliged, 'subject to this Act and in particular *section 15 (2) (d)*', to 'establish and maintain an admissions policy which provides for maximum accessibility to the school'.[37] The Act also obliges the Minister to recognise a school where the number 'attending or are likely to attend the school is such or is likely to be such as to make the school viable … having regard to the desirability of diversity in the classes of school operating in the area likely to be served by the school' and where 'the needs of students attending or likely to attend the school cannot reasonably be met by existing schools'.[38] A school board is obliged to

> (d) publish, in such manner as the board with the agreement of the patron considers appropriate, the policy of the school concerning admission to and participation in the school and … ensure that as regards that policy principles of equality and the right of parents to send their children to a school of the parents' choice are respected and such directions as may be made from time to time by the Minister, having

33. Ibid., Section 15 (2) (b).
34. Ibid., Section 30 (2) (b).
35. Ibid., Section 6 (a).
36. Ibid., Section 6 (e).
37. Ibid., Section 9 (m).
38. Ibid., Section 10 (2) (a) and (b).

regard to the characteristic spirit of the school and the constitutional rights of all persons concerned, are complied with,

(e) have regard to the principles and requirements of a democratic society and have respect and promote respect for the diversity of values, beliefs, traditions, languages and ways of life in society ... [39]

Two points emerge relevant to our purposes. The first concerns the rights of parents to have a choice of school. The possibility of making available alternatives to confessional schools for parents 'who do not have the option, for practical reasons, to select a school which reflects their particular choices'[40] is not seriously explored in the Green or White Papers.

Yet here I think it is important to distinguish between a guarantee that protects a negative freedom (i.e., it prevents the State from doing something) and a positive right (i.e., a requirement of the State to do something). The Constitution only commits the State to refrain from insisting that parents send their children to a particular school rather than conferring upon them a right to have available a school consistent with their preferences.[41]

We must also be circumspect in our use of the language of rights. The rhetoric of rights should not be promiscuously invoked in political discourse because, when we make a claim based on rights, we invoke particularly weighty and compelling moral considerations. As Loren Lomasky puts it, rights are the 'heavy artillery in our moral arsenal'[42] and there are limits to what

39. Ibid., Section 15 (2)(d) and (e).

40. Government of Ireland, *Charting Our Education Future: White Paper on Education*, p. 24.

41. I am grateful to Gerry Whyte for this clarification. See John Kelly, *The Irish Constitution*, edited by G. Hogan and G. Whyte 4th edition (Dublin: LexisNexis, 2003), 7.6. 294-297, pp. 1961-1963.

42. Loren Lomasky, *Persons, Rights and the Moral Community* (New York, Oxford University Press, 1987), p. 8. I explore the distinction between freedom and rights in a different context in Kevin Williams, 'Public Funds and Minority Broadcasting', in *The Media and the Marketplace: Ethical Perspectives,* eds. E. G. Cassidy and A.G. McGrady (Dublin: Institute of Public Administration, 2001), pp. 33-44.

can be demanded as a right, either as a liberty or as an entitlement.

We have to distinguish between freedom and rights and also between the right to education and the right to a particular kind of school. Children in Ireland have a right to education and parents have freedom to send their children to a school of their choice. But this does not mean that parents have a right, in the sense of an entitlement, to have a particular kind of school.

This limit upon rights is implied in the Education Act by reference to 'the effective and efficient use of resources'.[43] Accordingly, the State is not obliged to make available a nation-wide network of non-confessional schools or of any particular kind of school. Note, too, that the limit on the State's obligation in this respect would also apply to parental demands for confessional schools of a particular character.

To summarise: the obligation to ensure that children receive a primary education does not entail an obligation to ensure that parents have available to them a particular kind of school whether faith-based, multi-denominational, secular or other.

A second point concerns the tension at the heart of the Education Act 1998 between the right of patrons to main-tain a particular ethos and the principle of 'respect for the diversity of values, beliefs, traditions, languages and ways of life in society'[44] with regard to accommodating the children of parents who dissent from this ethos. This ethos pervades the curriculum and the whole life of the school; so, the right to withdraw from lessons in religion would not prevent children being exposed to religion.

This was made clear in the Supreme Court judgement in response to the challenge to the payment from public funds of chaplains in Community Schools. The essence of this challenge was that individuals were in receipt of state salaries in order to exercise denominational ministries directed at co-religionists in

43. Government of Ireland, *Education Act 1998*, Section 6 (e).
44. Ibid., Section 15 (d) and (e).

public institutions. Such payment was judged to be consistent with the Constitution.[45] The Court found that the right not to attend religious instruction could not protect a child 'from being influenced, to some degree, by the religious "ethos" of the school'.[46] Accordingly, school management is 'not obliged to change the general atmosphere of its school merely to accommodate a child of a differen™t religious persuasion who wishes to attend that school'[47]. But this does not affect the right to withdraw from Religious Education and, moreover, any attempt at proselytism is explicitly ruled out.[48] This means that parents who send their children to a school animated by different beliefs and values from theirs, whether these be religious or secular, cannot expect that school to change its ethos to affirm the beliefs that they wish to have fostered in their children.

This is consistent with the conditions in two other legislative instruments. The first is the Employment Equality Act 1998 which states:

> 37. – (1) A religious, educational or medical institution which is under the direction or control of a body established for religious purposes or whose objectives include the provision of services in an environment which promotes certain religious values shall not be taken to discriminate against a person for the purposes of this Part or *Part II* if–
>
> (*a*) it gives more favourable treatment, on the religion ground, to an employee or a prospective employee over that person where it is reasonable to do so in order to maintain the religious ethos of the institution, or
>
> (*b*) it takes action which is reasonably necessary to prevent

45. See Campaign to Separate Church and State Ltd and Jeremiah Noel Murphy v Minister for Education, the Attorney General, The Most Reverend Cathal Daly, The Most Reverend Desmond Connell, The Most Reverend Dermot Clifford and the Most Reverend Joseph Cassidy: Supreme Court 1996 No. 36 (Hamilton CJ. O'Flaherty, Denham, Barrington and Keane JJ) 25 March 1998 (*Nem Diss.*) *Irish Law Review Monthly*, 2 (1998), pp. 81-101.

46. Ibid. p. 101

47. Ibid.

48. Ibid.

an employee or a prospective employee from undermining the religious ethos of the institution.[49]

A previous draft (1996) was much stronger. Sub-clause (a) excluded 'discrimination' where 'essential for the maintenance of the religious ethos of the institution or is reasonable to avoid offending the religious sensitivities of its members or clients'.[50] The section now reflects the requirement in Community Schools that a 'teacher shall not advertently and consistently seek to undermine the religious belief or practice of any pupil in the school'.[51]

The other piece of legislation relevant to this issue appears in the Equal Status Act 2000, Section 7 (3) (C). A charge of discrimination does not apply

> (c) where the establishment is a school providing primary or post-primary education to students and the objective of the school is to provide education in an environment which promotes certain religious values, it admits persons of a particular religious denomination in preference to others or it refuses to admit as a student a person who is not of that denomination and, in the case of a refusal, it is proved that the refusal is essential to maintain the ethos of the school.[52]

In the absence of guidelines for good practice, these Acts provide only general principles regarding any possible tension that might arise between the rights of patrons and the rights of parents who dissent form the ethos of the school. By contrast, the Education Act did allow the State become involved in the provision and assessment of Religious Education.[53] This initia-

49. Government of Ireland, *Employment Equality Act 1998* (Dublin: The Stationery Office, 1998), Section 37 (1).

50. Government of Ireland, *Employment Equality Bill 1996* (Dublin: The Stationery Office, 1996), 37 (1) (b).

51. Association of Community Schools, Model Lease for Community Schools (Dublin: Association of Community Schools, 1992), 7D, p. 22.

52. Government of Ireland, *Equal Status Act 2000* (Dublin: The Stationery Office, 2000), Section 7 (3) (C).

53. Government of Ireland, *Education Act 1998,* Part IV, 35.

tive, to which we turn in the next chapter, does answer concerns regarding the catechetical character of Religious Education at second-level.

CHAPTER FOUR

Religious Education
and the State

One concrete outcome of the Education Act was the removal of the prohibition on examining Religious Education. This allowed the introduction of a new syllabus in Religious Education sponsored and assessed under the direction of the Department of Education. As a result a greater spirit of inclusiveness has come to inform the treatment of religion in education at second level. In introducing this spirit of inclusiveness into Religious Education, the area had first to be distinguished from cognate areas of moral and civic education.

RELIGIOUS EDUCATION AND COGNATE AREAS

Until the 1990s there had, unfortunately, been no clear consideration of the relationship between religious, moral, values education and health education. Until 1995, which saw the introduction of Relationships and Sexuality Education at both primary and second levels, there was no mandatory provision for direct values education at primary level. At second level, the study of civics was compulsory for all junior cycle pupils but, regrettably, there had not been a tradition of taking the subject seriously and there were (and still are) no requirements regarding the qualifications necessary to teach it. This meant that general moral/values education of a formal nature had traditionally been included within the remit of Religious Education. In fact, it might be argued that the emphasis within Religious Education had become insufficiently theological due to the need to incorporate subject matter that more appropriately belonged in civics and in programmes of personal and social development. This tendency was reinforced by Religious Education being a non-examined subject. Many schools perceived religion class as the location for the promotion of the personal development that it was not possible to provide within the constraints of the curriculum dominated by the demands of examinations.

Clarification of the relationship between religious education and personal, social and moral education was also necessary to highlight the obligation of the State under Article 42 of the Constitution to ensure that every pupil receive a 'certain minimum education, moral, intellectual and social'. This would draw attention to the formal provision required to secure the general moral education of pupils who were withdrawn from religious instruction.

The trend of government policy has been to assign the broader remit of values education to health education. Both the Green and White Papers attributed to health education the main role in the formation of personal and social values, including what are referred to in the former document as 'spiritual values'.

The promotion of health and well-being were envisaged as occurring within the context of 'the wider educational and spiritual values transmitted by the school'.[1] One of the elements mentioned under health promotion was sexuality education, which clearly involves consideration of values. In the Green Paper a programme in sexuality education was listed as one of the defining features of the health-promoting school and it was recommended that it be provided at a level appropriate to all pupils, beginning in the early stages of primary education.[2] Health promotion in schools was assigned an explicit moral remit. The Green Paper referred to helping students to 'become young persons who are honest, direct and self-confident, yet sensitive to the feelings and rights of others' and the White Paper referred to fostering 'integrity, self-confidence and self-esteem while nurturing sensitivity to the feelings and rights of others'.[3]

1. Government of Ireland, *Education for A Changing World: Green Paper on Education*, p. 129.

2. *Education for A Changing World: Green Paper on Education*, pp. 12/13, 129-131.

3. Ibid. p. 129; Government of Ireland, *Charting Our Education Future: White Paper on Education*, p. 161.

Consistent with the policy of assigning the broader remit of values education to health education, formal arrangements were proposed for the teaching of Relationships and Sexuality Education (RSE) in primary and second level schools in January 1995. In the document introducing the new arrangements, the Minister for Education also announced that hours spent teaching RSE would count for salaried purposes. It is interesting to note the high profile given to the moral and spiritual dimension of this aspect of education. The third paragraph of the document stated:

> Through Relationships and Sexuality Education, formal opportunities are provided for young people to acquire knowledge and understanding of human sexuality, through processes which will enable them to form values and establish behaviours within a moral and spiritual framework.[4]

Further on, the document stated that RSE would 'be determined and delivered in accordance with the ethos and core values of the individual school'.[5] The document also asked that each school 'make provision for the right of parents who hold conscientious or moral objections to the inclusion of such programmes on the curriculum' and required of school authorities that they 'state how the school intends to address these situations'.[6] As we have seen in the preceding chapter, this affirmation of the right of schools is consistent with the provisions of the Education Act.

Subsequently, RSE was incorporated into Social, Personal and Health Education (SPHE). This was included in the primary curriculum (1999) and is to become an subject for assessment for the Junior Certificate. The other explicit element of values education to be considered next is Civics.

---

4. Department of Education, Circular Letter M4/95: Relationships and Sexuality Education (Dublin: Department of Education, 1995), p. 1.
   5. Ibid, p. 4.
   6. Ibid.

CIVIC EDUCATION

The old subject 'Civics' was to enjoy a change in title and in profile in 1996 with the introduction of Civic, Social and Political Education (CSPE) as a subject for the Junior Certificate. The professsionalisation of the area has led to a welcome energy and focus in the teaching of the subject. And its introduction at senior cycle is a serious possibility.

The new syllabus for CSPE marks a change in policy towards the profile of religion in civic education. The notion of tolerance mentioned in 1966 emerges as a defining element of the document on Civic, Social and Political Education at second level, published in 1996.[7] This document endorses the secular values of liberal democracy and also places a very strong emphasis on communitarian values of social responsibility. What is significant is the failure even to raise the possibility of a connection between religion and civic education. In a country where religion and culture have been so intimately related, this neglect is very surprising. Whether this is a result of a considered change in policy or of an unselfconscious response to a new *Zeitgeist* is difficult to say, although I am inclined towards the latter explanation.

The salience of religion in Irish culture makes it a topic that should be included in any officially-sponsored programme of civic education. Religion is a very significant feature in the political division of the island as well as having a place in the cultural self-understanding of both believers and non-believers. In Chapters One and Two, the manifold expressions of the relationship between faith and culture in Ireland were noted.

To this we should add the role of the Church in raising awareness of disadvantage and exploitation. The missionary Church has animated much of the contribution of Ireland to the developing world and has highlighted poverty and exploitation in these areas of the world. No doubt there were Irish religious

7. Department of Education, *The Junior Certificate: Civic, Social and Political Education Syllabus* (Dublin: The Stationery Office, 1996).

involved in the opposition to Pinochet in Chile referred to in Chapter One. Gene Kerrigan captures this aspect of the remit of Christianity by pointing out that it was inspiration from the Gospel that 'created the men and women, priests and nuns, volunteers, who went to the godforsaken spots of the globe to bear witness to finer values than accommodation to the local thug or dictator'.[8] Others, he writes, 'stayed home and stood by the oppressed or spoke out against the complacency of the comfortable classes'.[9] The ideals of human conduct enshrined in the Christian tradition (in the parable of the Good Samaritan or in the Sermon on the Mount, for example) form part of the moral capital of our civic culture. Indeed, a close connection exists between the values which are promoted in the CSPE programme (human dignity, interdependence and stewardship, for example) and Christian values in general.

The syllabus in Religious Education, by contrast, has an explicit civic remit. One of its aims is to prepare students for 'the responsibilities of citizenship' by exploring the 'unique role' of the Christian tradition 'and its denominational expressions in Irish life'.[10] This syllabus also has a section dealing with the place of religion in civil life.[11] So it is surprising there is not a parallel treatment of the theme in the CSPE programme. This is not to say that we should return to the pious over-emphasis on religion of previous documents. But the Judaeo-Christian story has played such a role in shaping the national psyche that it should be incorporated into the civic story of the country.

This takes us to the treatment of Religious Education (RE) itself.

8. G. Kerrigan, *Another Country: Growing up in '50s Ireland* (Dublin: Gill and Macmillan, 1998), p. 118.

9. Ibid. It seems to me, though, that of the concern for the poor voiced by radical clergy of past has been mainstreamed. The urgency with which they spoke has been domesticated into moralising rhetoric by some clergy today.

10. Department of Education and Science, *Religious Education Syllabus: Ordinary and Higher Level* (Dublin: The Stationery Office, 2000), p. 4.

11. Ibid., p. 43.

THE CHARACTER OF RELIGIOUS EDUCATION

As we have seen, the repeal in the Education Act of a rule in the Intermediate Education Act of 1878 prohibiting examinations in religion allowed for the introduction of Religious Education as a subject for state examinations at second level. Facilitated by the commitment and vision of former and current senior personnel in the National Council for Curriculum and Assessment, the subject is now established at Junior Cycle level and is being introduced as a Leaving Certificate subject. It is worth dwelling in some detail on the character of this syllabus because it captures much that is positive in the spirit of contemporary policy on the role of religion in education.

The rationale for the Religious Education (RE) curriculum is inclusive and consistent with liberal democratic principles.

> From the earliest times, the experience of the spiritual and the human search for meaning have frequently found expression in a religious interpretation of life. The history of humanity has been indelibly marked by the contributions of religious traditions. In Ireland, Christianity is part of our rich cultural heritage and has played a significant role in shaping our vision of ourselves., our world and our relationships with others. However, effective functioning in an increasingly complex culture demands that people have an understanding of a variety of religious traditions and an appreciation of the richness of the major religious traditions encountered not just in Ireland but in Europe and the wider world. Increasingly, modern culture also calls for engagement with the secular response to human experience.[12]

The document goes on to affirm the role of Religious Education in enabling young people critically to reflect upon and to interpret human experience.

> Religious Education should ensure that students are exposed to a broad range of religious traditions and to the non-

12. Ibid., p. 3.

religious interpretation of life. It has a particular role to play
in the curriculum in the promotion of tolerance and mutual
understanding. It seeks to develop in students the skills
needed to engage in meaningful dialogue with those of other,
or of no, religious traditions.[13]

Religious Education is envisaged as 'offering opportunities to
develop an informed and critical understanding of the Christian
tradition in its historical origins and its cultural and social
expressions'[14] as part of the overall remit of the curriculum in
promoting the capacity to think critically. This critical spirit also
informs its moral compass. By introducing 'a variety of ethical
codes and norms for behaviour', Religious Education aims to
encourage students to

> engage critically with these moral systems in an effort to arrive
> at a thought-through moral stance that will serve as a founda-
> tion for the decisions they will face as adults and for the
> patterns of behaviour and commitment that will mark how
> they will relate to their local communities and to the world in
> general.[15]

When it comes to the general aim of RE, the same principles
are evident. The principal aim is 'to provide students with a
framework for encountering and engaging with the variety of
religious traditions in Ireland and elsewhere'.[16] The aims also
highlight the importance of experience in education and of
reflection on this experience. In the light of this, the commitment of young people 'to a particular religious tradition, and /
or to a continuing search for meaning' is to be 'encouraged and
supported'.[17] Critics of the syllabus should also note that it gives
ample scope for searching and detailed study of Christianity as

12. Ibid., p. 3.
13. Ibid., p. 4.
14. Ibid.
15. Ibid.
16. Ibid.
17. Ibid.

expressed in its different traditions. It also 'seeks to promote an understanding and appreciation of why people believe, as well as tolerance and respect for the values and beliefs of all'.[18] And as we have just seen, one of the aims of RE is to prepare students for citizenship by exploring the 'unique role' of the Christian tradition 'and its denominational expressions in Irish life'.[19]

It is worth noting the summary enunciation of the aims of Religious Education.

- To foster an awareness that the human search for meaning is common to all peoples, of all ages and at all times
- To explore how this search for meaning has found, and continues to find, expression in religion
- To identify how understanding of God, religious traditions, and in particular the Christian tradition, have contributed to the culture in which we live, and continue to have an impact on personal life-style, inter-personal relationships and relationships between individuals and their communities and contexts
- To appreciate the richness of religious traditions and to acknowledge the non-religious interpretation of life
- To contribute to the spiritual and moral development of the student.[20]

This approach to RE demonstrates the educational value of having it as part of the curriculum. As shall be argued more fully in Chapter Six, any education that claims to be comprehensive demands that young people be given an opportunity to acquire some kind of experience of religion from the inside.[21] This is necessary to enable young people both to acquire a sense of what

18. Ibid.
19. Ibid.
20. Ibid., p. 5.
21. In Régis Debray's *L'Enseignement du Fait Religieux dans L'École Laïque* (Paris: Editions Odile Jacob, 2002), the author offers two striking expressions of what is meant by the experience of religion from the inside. He speaks of it as '*un engagement vécu de l'intérieur qui fait corps avec la personne même*', pp. 22/23 ('an involvement lived from within that becomes part of the individual') and '*le cœur battant de la foi vécue*', p. 40 '(the beating heart of living faith').

it means to hold a religious belief and also to enable them to appreciate the religious dimension of general culture. The Irish approach demonstrates the possibility of designing a course that is theologically, culturally and personally enriching and at the same time respectful of the beliefs of all. It has many of the positive features of the approach to religion in Norway that shall be considered again in the Conclusion to this volume.

Besides conferring on the subject a status that it did not previously enjoy, public examinations in Religious Education should have the somewhat paradoxical benefit of reinforcing the theological dimension of religious education. This is because the syllabus for examinations in religion can concentrate on conventional theological subject-matter rather than on material which can be covered in programmes of personal and social development. Of course, I would not wish to deny the implications of religious belief for moral education and for full personal development. But the primary concern of Religious Education is with the spiritual realm of human experience and its primary purpose is to enable young people to deepen their sensitivity and response to the transcendent action of God in their lives. In order to deepen the response of young people to the action of God in their lives, it is important to concentrate on subject-matter which is explicitly and directly theological rather on material which would find a more appropriate place in CSPE or Geography class or in programmes of personal and social development.

THE NEW CONTEXT FOR RELIGIOUS EDUCATION: RESERVATIONS

I next wish to make some comments on the fear that state assessment in Religious Education may result in religion being treated as simply another examination subject. I am optimistic that the introduction of religion as an examination subject will not lead to the neglect of the non-examinable aspects of religious belief and practice. After all, S0tate examinations in religion have been a feature of education in Northern Ireland and it is unlikely that the catechetical formation of young people in the

Northern part of our island is inferior to that in the Republic. The commitment of those who manage and teach in our schools makes me confident that our educators are not likely to mistake the study of religion for a genuine encounter with religion as an integral aspect of human living. The case for making religion an examination subject may become clearer if we distinguish the multiple contexts in which Religious Education takes place and further distinguish between the practical and theoretical dimensions of Religious Education.

Education, Schooling and the Curriculum

Firstly we need to distinguish between education, schooling and the curriculum. Education refers to all that which has been designed for the purpose of teaching us something. Schools are not the only institutions that provide education in general and Religious Education in particular. Education, religious and secular, occurs within the family and parish and at times through the media.

Schooling, which refers to the normal institutional arrangement made for the education of young people, is one particular context within which education takes place.

The curriculum refers to prescribed, learnable activities, which are contained in a syllabus, and which normally are assessed. Although it is probably the main focus of a school's activities, not all learning occurs *via* the formal curriculum. Young people learn through the experience of living as part of the school community. The state syllabus in Religious Education is not therefore the only encounter young people will have with religion. Apart from any lessons of a direct catechetical nature, Religious Education can also be a significant feature of their experience of the school's culture. This education occurs through the experience of a school's ethos, which is the embodiment of the school's culture. This ethos is imparted through the spirit of the school – through the staff, through the profile given to the symbols of religious belief, through the place given to prayer, worship and liturgy.

We need also to distinguish carefully between the practical and theoretical dimensions of Religious Education.

Religious Education: Its Practical and Theoretical Dimensions

The practical dimension of religion refers to a way of apprehending the world and of living. This involves a disposition, mind-set, or state of mind composed of a matrix of beliefs, convictions, attitudes, feelings and emotions regarding humankind's place in the universe and ultimate fate. This disposition is commonly expressed in acts of worship or prayer and also in the form of moral commitments to act in ways that are consistent with realising this ultimate destiny.

The theoretical dimension of religion, on the other hand, has several different aspects, both as subject matter in its own right and as part of the subject matter of other disciplines. In the first place, we have the doctrines of religious faith expressed as a series of propositions or creed. This is the theory of religious belief at its least sophisticated level as it consists only in the straightforward propositions of doctrine as they can be expressed systematically. Secondly, we have the theories about creedal propositions provided by theologians. These theories explore the nature and content of the creedal statements but they do not normally call into question the philosophical basis of these statements. (At these two levels we are speaking of religion as subject matter in its own right.) Thirdly, there are theories about theology provided by philosophers and historians. These theories do call into question the logical/epistemological status of religious beliefs (religion as the subject matter of other disciplines). Finally, there are theories about religious belief as a phenomenon in human life and society. These are the theories about religion offered by the human sciences of psychology, sociology, anthropology and geography.

And there is no doubt that in principle the theoretical dimension of religious belief both as subject matter in its own right (levels one and two) and as part of the subject matter of other disciplines (levels three and four) can be examined. As noted in

Chapter Two, in the past concern with formulated doctrines and principles tended to be given priority over the initiation of young people into the religious way of apprehending life and of living. Yet Christianity must be put in systematic doctrinal form if young people are to understand the faith which they have inherited and, indeed, if they are to give reason to outsiders for the faith that is in them. Moreover, knowledge of the intellectual basis of faith can also deepen and enrich the quality of religious experience.

Examinations in religion are concerned with the theoretical dimension of religious belief. But this does not mean that this is all that there is to religion or that this is all that schools should be concerned with. Teaching young people propositions about religious belief cannot communicate to them the lived richness of a religious tradition or way of life. Understanding such propositions is certainly no substitute for religious experience. It is simply not possible to assess the quality of a person's religious experience; neither is it appropriate to assess participation in liturgical life. But the theoretical aspect of religion can be taught and learned in a form amenable to assessment, and in the examination it is this theoretical dimension alone that is being assessed.

BELIEF AND NON-BELIEF ACROSS THE CURRICULUM:
THE ROLE OF LITERATURE

I wish to conclude by reference to possible reservations about the profile being given to non-religious worldviews in the new course in Religious Education. It has always been necessary in any education worthy of the name that young people encounter such views. Liberal democratic and educational principles require that teachers of religion in confessional contexts deal honestly with secular worldviews. As John Stuart Mill comments: 'If Christians would teach infidels to be just to Christianity, they should themselves be just to infidelity'.[22] In any case, in so far as Religious

22. John Stuart Mill, *On Liberty*, in *Mill*, Norton Critical Edition, Alan Ryan, ed., New York/London: W.W. Norton, 1997, p. 81.

Education in Ireland is concerned with cultivating the imaginative capacities of young to connect with the Christian story, it must also leave room for an imaginative dwelling with other narratives regarding the meaning and purpose of life.

Let also us bear in mind that encountering different worldviews has always been a feature of studying literature. It is true that the primary purpose is to of teaching literature is to equip us to enjoy what Harold Bloom describes as the 'difficult pleasure' of reading well.[23]

But literature can also prompt us to review critically beliefs and attitudes that we hold dear. Reading well, as Bloom reminds with reference to the advice of Samuel Johnson, challenges us 'not to contradict and confute, nor to believe and take for granted, ... but to weigh and consider' what we read in respect of how to make sense of the world and even to acquire knowledge 'not just of self and others, but of the way things are'.[24] To adapt the famous expression of Kant's with regard to his reading of David Hume, literature can awaken us out of our 'dogmatic slumbers'.[25]

Brendan Kennelly expresses this potential of literature very well: 'Poems that work get to the root of your position, they insist on becoming central to your life and may even change it'.[26] Such poetry 'reads you' in the sense that it 'really forces you to look at yourself' operating like a 'time bomb in the guts of complacency'.[27]

Drawing on his study of the journals of Gerard Manley Hopkins, Denis Donoghue rightly argues that the purpose of reading literature is to cultivate an 'ability to imagine being different' and

23. Harold Bloom, *How to Read and Why* (London: Fourth Estate, 2001), p. 29.

24. Op. cit., pp. 21, 29. The first quotation is taken by Bloom from Johnson and the second is Bloom's own.

25. This expression occurs in the Introduction to Immanuel Kant, *Prolegomena to Any Future Metaphysics* (New York: MacMillan, 1950).

26. This quotation is taken from part of an interview with Brendan Kennelly in Siobhán McSweeney, 'The Poets' Picture of Education', *The Crane Bag*, vol. 7, no. 2 (1983), pp. 134-142, p. 140.

27. These quotations from Kennelly are taken from Daniel Murphy, *Education and the Arts* (Dublin: School of Education, Trinity College, Dublin, 1987), p. 54.

'to project myself into the state of being of another person.'[28] The experience of reading should 'provoke me to imagine what it would mean to have a life different from my own'.[29]

Or consider the account of the potential of literature to subvert our usual ways of understanding the word in Azar Nafisi's *Reading Lolita in Tehran: A Memoir in Books*. Gathering a group of former students to read forbidden works of Western literature, Nafisi demonstrates how encounters with fictional worlds encouraged the students in their opposition to the theocratic totalitarianism of Iran in the 1990s. '[M]ost great works of the imagination,' writes Nafisi, are 'meant to make you feel like a stranger in your own home'.[30] They prompt us to question what we take for granted, especially 'traditions and expectations' where they appear 'immutable'.[31] She invites her students to consider the way in which great literature unsettles them, makes them 'a little uneasy' and invites them 'to look around and consider the world, like Alice in Wonderland, through different eyes'.[32] What a novel offers, she writes, is

> the sensual experience of another world. If you don't enter that world, hold your breath with the characters and become involved in their destiny, you won't be able to empathize, and empathy is at the heart of the novel. This is how you read a novel: you inhale the experience.[33]

This means that any school curriculum that includes the teaching of literature must *ipso facto* accommodate a serious engagement with different worldviews. Students must learn 'to inhale' different experiences and to go beyond 'control beliefs', that is, ideological predispositions that inhibit a properly gener-

28. Denis Donoghue, *The Practice of Reading* (New Haven and London: Yale University Press, 1998), p. 56.

29. Ibid.

30. Azar Nafisi, *Reading Lolita in Tehran: A Memoir in Books* (London and New York: Fourth Estate, 2004), p. 94.

31. Ibid.

32. Ibid.

33. Ibid., p. 111.

ous reading of texts.[34] To draw on an insight of Eva Hoffman's,[35] literature is animated by a powerful democratising impulse, which means that every reader encounters a text on equal terms regardless of beliefs and background. In this way the teaching of literature subverts the aspiration to moral and ideological protectionism in education. But also, as I hope to show in Chapter Six, this teaching also serves to subvert certain conceptions of the neutral teacher.

As challenges to religious belief are not uncommon in literature, teaching it young people whithin contexts where religion is part of the belief system of home and school requires enabling them to enter imaginatively into secular mindsets. By the same token, to teach literature to young people who are being taught in secular contexts, whatever the upbringing of the home, requires enabling them to acquire a sense of what it means to hold a religious belief. But this is an issue for another context.[36]

Teaching literature always demands sensitivity and skill in enabling learners to enter imaginatively into different worldviews. As Nafisi's memoir demonstrates, the attempt to exercise religious control over imaginative literature is folly. From a practical point of view, censorship is unworkable; from an educational point of view, it is reprehensible; and from the point of view of faith development, it is counter-productive. For example, I do not think that anyone would seriously argue that young people should be prohibited from reading *Portrait of the Artist as a Young Man* because the novel describes the protagonist, Stephen Dedalus, rejecting Catholicism.

Or let us take two other examples in more detail. In John

34. I am grateful to David I. Smith for alerting me to this expression that he has used in his work of the reading theory of N. Wolstertorff.

35. See Eva Hoffman, *Lost In Translation: A Life in a New Language* (London: Vintage, 1998), p. 183 where she speaks of the 'democratizing power' of literature.

36. The educational imperatives that arise when teaching literature informed by religious beliefs in secular contexts are explored in detail in Kevin Williams, 'The Religious Dimension of Cultural Initiation: Has It a Place in a Secular World?', *Ethical Perspectives*, vol. 11, no. 4 (December 2004), pp. 228-37.

McGahern's novel, *That They May Face the Rising Sun*, a discussion takes place early in the first chapter about going to Mass. One character does not attend because he does not believe and would feel a hypocrite if he went to Mass. Another replies ' "None of us believes and we go. That's no bar" '.[37] Again I do not think that anyone would seriously defend a prohibition on young people reading the novel on account of this passage. Rather than discouraging young people from reading it, what the teacher needs to do is to enable the students to connect with the mindset that informs both characters. This will require enabling them to understand the non-religious perspective on life and helping them to appreciate that faith should involve more than mere conformity to a social and cultural norm.

Likewise, it would not be wise to try to prevent young people from reading Roddy Doyle's *A Star Called Henry*, on account of the incident where the eponymous hero trenchantly disparages religion in general and Christianity in particular.[38] Here again a teacher should rather invite students imaginatively to enter into the experiences that led to such a negative reaction to religion in order to understand that the reaction was in part a response on the part of a child to neglect and unkindness.

We should also bear in mind that encounters with different worldviews also occur in the course of the study of history – for example, in learning about the Reformation or about the Age of Enlightenment or about Church-State tensions in France. The study of both history and literature can extend and enlarge our capacities to understand the beliefs, motivations and behaviour of other people. As encounters with other worldviews normally take place across the curriculum, therefore the systematic treatment in Religious Education of these views is quite appropriate. These encounters are educationally appropriate, indeed necessary. This point is captured powerfully in the famous passage of John Stuart Mill's *On Liberty*.

37. John McGahern, *That They May Face the Rising Sun* (London: Faber and Faber, 2003), p. 2.
38. Roddy Doyle, *A Star Called Henry* (London: Jonathan Cape, 1999), p. 79.

He who knows only is own side of the case, knows little of that. His reasons may be good, and no one may be able to refute them. But if he is equally unable to refute the reasons on the opposite side; if he does not so much as know what they are, he has no ground for preferring either opinion.[39]

Unless people encounter contrary views 'in their most plausible and persuasive form' and have 'thrown themselves into the mental position of those who think differently from them, and considered what such persons may have to say . . . they do not in any proper sense of the word, know the doctrine which they themselves profess'.[40] People in this situation end up either following authority or embracing the point of view to which they simply feel 'most inclination'.[41]

It is then intellectually appropriate to give a profile given to different views in the Religious Education syllabus. By giving a profile to these views in RE at second level, the State also facilitates a reconciliation between the Christian tradition and the demands of diversity. The achievement of a similar reconciliation at primary level has proved more problematic – as we shall see in the chapter that follows.

39. Mill, *On Liberty*, p. 69.
40. Ibid.
41. Ibid.

CHAPTER FIVE

Tradition and Pluralism in the Primary Curriculum[1]

A new, more inclusive direction in government policy is to be found in the revised version of the document on the primary school curriculum.[2] The document affirms the significance for most Irish people of a religious perspective on life but, like the Education Act, it does not commit the State to a direct endorsement of the Christian view of human destiny. It is therefore no longer State policy to expect all schools to subscribe to the same worldview. Consistent with the Act, it then becomes a matter for individual school communities whether or not they wish to promote an ethos reflecting the Christian view of life. Yet the problem remains of accommodating the wishes of parents who do not wish their children to encounter faith-based worldviews but who have no realistic alternative to confessional schools.[3] Nonetheless, the spirit and tone of the aims of the Primary Curriculum published in 1999 are very different from those of its 1971 predecessor. Let us therefore examine these aims.

THE AIMS OF THE NEW PRIMARY CURRICULUM

In the 1999 document we read that one of fourteen issues on which there was 'consensus' among those drafting the text was the place of 'the spiritual dimension in life' as well as of 'plural-

---

1. An earlier version of this chapter appeared under the title 'Pluralism and the Christian Tradition in the New (1999) Primary Curriculum', *REA/Religion, Education and the Arts*, 4 (2003), pp. 30-38.

2. Department of Education and Science, *The Primary Curriculum: Introduction* (Dublin: The Stationery Office, 1999).

3. It would be hard to give exact figures regarding the numbers involved. The recent INTO document does give some information regarding percentage of children whose parents do not share the faith of the school. See Irish National Teachers' Organisation, *Teaching Religion in the Primary School: Issues and Challenges* (Dublin: Irish National Teachers' Organisation, 2003), p. 50.

ism, a respect for diversity and the importance of tolerance'.[4] The
following are some affirmations of respect for diversity. Under
the heading 'European and Global Dimensions', the authors
state:

> The curriculum acknowledges, too, the importance of a
> balanced and informed awareness of the diversity of peoples
> and environments in the world. Such an awareness helps
> children to understand the world and contributes to their
> personal and social development as citizens of a global com-
> munity.[5]

This is consistent with the character of 'Social, Environmental
and Scientific Education' which is described as follows:

> ...as children mature they encounter a widening range of
> people, events and periods. These are drawn from local,
> national, European and non-European contexts and from
> diverse social, cultural, ethnic and religious backgrounds, so
> that children acquire a balanced understanding of local, Irish
> and international history.[6]

One of the features of 'Social, Personal and Health Education' is that it will nurture '[c]oncepts of democracy, justice and
inclusiveness ... through the learning experiences offered and
through the attitudes and practices inherent in the organisational structures of the class and the school'. [7]

This endorsement of the importance of understanding and
tolerating diversity is unlikely to be contested. The practical
implications of respecting diversity are more complex and are
fraught with potential disagreement. Indeed, as I propose to
show, the very drafting of the document reflects the sensitivity of
the undertaking.

4. Department of Education and Science, *The Primary Curriculum: Introduction*,
p. 9.
   5. Ibid., p. 27.
   6. Ibid., p. 49.
   7. Ibid., p. 57.

RESPONDING TO PLURALISM AND DIVERSITY

Let us examine, first, what is said under the heading 'Pluralism'.

> The curriculum has a particular responsibility in promoting tolerance and respect for diversity in both the school and the community. Children come from a diversity of cultural, religious, social, environmental and ethnic backgrounds, and these engender their own beliefs, values, and aspirations. The curriculum acknowledges the centrality of the Christian heritage and tradition in the Irish experience and the Christian identity shared by the majority of Irish people. It equally recognises the diversity of beliefs, values and aspirations of all religious and cultural groups in society.[8]

According to the draft version (quotations from this version are given in italics) of the document reported in *The Irish Times*, the Christian aspect of Irish culture was not mentioned.

> *Draft: The curriculum acknowledges this pluralism in society and caters for a variety of differences while at the same time promoting tolerance and respect for diversity in both the school and the community.*[9]

This leads to the very sensitive matter of the role of religion in the curriculum where, again, the draft differs from the final version. In the final version, under 'The Spiritual Dimension', we read that the 'curriculum takes cognisance of the affective, aesthetic, spiritual, moral and religious dimensions of the child's experience and development'.[10] According to the draft, reference seems to have been made only to '*the spiritual dimension in the child's overall development*'.[11] The broad sense in which 'spiritual' is used in both versions seems to embrace forms of spiritual

9. Andy Pollack, 'New School Curriculum Leaves out God in Favour of Spiritual Dimension', *The Irish Times*, 22 August 1998, p. 4.

10. Department of Education and Science, *The Primary Curriculum: Introduction*, p. 27.

11. Pollack, 'New School Curriculum Leaves out God in Favour of Spiritual Dimension.

experience that are not connected to religious traditions and consequently implies that the spiritual and religious spheres do not have to be related. The paragraph in the final version continues:

> For most people in Ireland, the totality of the human condition cannot be understood or explained merely in terms of physical and social experience. This conviction comes from a shared perception that intimates a more profound explanation of being, from an awareness of the finiteness of life and from the sublime fulfilment that human existence sometimes affords. The spiritual dimension of life expresses itself in a search for truth and in the quest for a transcendent element within human experience.[12]

In the draft version the word '*many*' rather than 'most' appears. The draft paragraph reads as follows:

> *Draft: For many people the totality of the human condition cannot be understood or explained merely in terms of physical and social experience. The belief in a further dimension of human existence springs from a sense of the inadequacy of even the fullest explanation of life and its purpose solely in terms of experience and observation, and from a shared experience that intimates a more profound explanation of being. The quest and desire for such a transcendental element in human existence encompasses* [sic] *the spiritual dimension of life and finds* [sic] *fulfilment in many ways.* [13]

In the final version, the section on the 'Spiritual Dimension' concludes with an attempt to explain what it includes:

> The importance that the curriculum attributes to the child's spiritual development is expressed through the breadth of learning experiences the curriculum offers, through the inclusion of religious education as one of the areas of the

12. Department of Education and Science, *The Primary Curriculum: Introduction*, p. 27.

13. Pollack, 'New School Curriculum Leaves out God in Favour of Spiritual Dimension'.

curriculum, and through the child's engagement with the aesthetic and affective domains of learning.[14]

The final version of the document affirms the religious element of the spiritual dimension of life but it is not clear whether this was envisaged in the draft version.

SPIRITUALITY: WHAT DOES IT MEAN?

As we have seen, one of fourteen issues on which there was 'consensus' among those drafting the document *The Primary School Curriculum* was the place of 'the spiritual dimension in life'. Unfortunately, the term is not examined in any detail in spite of the voluminous literature on the subject.[15] The failure to explain what spirituality means is disappointing and it is worth commenting briefly on the notion here, and on the relationship between religion and spirituality. There are religious and secular versions of spirituality, although these domains do not have clear boundaries and even the very notion of religion is not clear-cut. We can identify six main aspects of spirituality, and closer examination will reveal the differences and similarities between spirituality and religion.

Underlying the six aspects is the non-instrumental and non-utilitarian character of spirituality. By this is meant that being spiritual is not connected to earning a living or survival or what, in his poem, 'The World Is Too Much with Us', Wordsworth describes as the world of 'getting and spending'. Spirituality relates to a quality of life that lies beyond the mere fact of living, to a world 'beyond utility'.[16] The spiritual and the ascetic are

14. Department of Education and Science, *The Primary Curriculum: Introduction*, p. 27.

15. A recent, extensive examination of the notion of spirituality in education can be found in D. Carr and J. Haldane, eds., *Spirituality, Philosophy and Education* (London: RoutledgeFalmer, 2003). A shorter account of the area, on which I draw for this section, can be found in Hanan Alexander and T.H. McLaughlin, 'Education in Religion and Spirituality' in *The Blackwell Guide to Philosophy of Education*, ed., Nigel Blake et al. (Oxford: Blackwell, 2003), pp. 356-373.

16. I have adapted the distinction between the quality and fact of life from A. N. Whitehead, *Religion in the Making* (Cambridge: Cambridge University Press, 1926), p. 80 and the expression 'beyond utility' is taken from Mary McCarthy, *Memories of a Catholic Childhood* (Harmondworth, London: Penguin, 1967), p. 26.

related because, as with asceticism, spirituality involves a detachment from bodily needs and desires.

The first strand of spirituality concerns the search or quest for meaning. In religious terms, the quest for meaning takes place within a tradition of belief and discourse about what is ultimate and what gives purpose to human life. This normally means God and the afterlife. In the secular version, this quest for meaning is reflected in a sense that there is more to life than appears on the surface and it is captured in the title of the U2 song, 'I Still Haven't Found What I'm Looking for'.

The second and third strands of the spiritual link it to the moral life. Strand two refers to its manifestation in personal qualities, and strand three concerns its collective or communal dimension. The personal qualities of the spiritual disposition include self-knowledge, self-control, self-possession, self-transcendence, calmness, love, generosity, trust, hope, wisdom, serenity, openness, humility and many more. These qualities have a moral character related to making the individual a better person and the world a better place. Significantly, too, relationships of friendship, love and affection, where the individuals involved are concerned only with the enjoyment of one another and where thoughts of usefulness do not apply, can be said to have a spiritual quality. The spiritual disposition or psychological orientation can be found in individuals of both religious and secular convictions and should not be identified solely with the former.

The collective or communal dimension of spirituality concerns the celebration of a sense of belonging, shared memory and commitment to a common purpose. This has very clear religious and secular expressions. Denominational services represent the most obvious religious version of this dimension of spirituality and some sporting occasions represent one secular version. In both contexts the expression of spirituality takes the form of communal bonding

The fourth strand of the spiritual refers to feelings of awe, reverence and wonder in response to the human and natural world. Clearly these feelings can take religious and secular forms. From both secular and religious perspectives, creation is quite properly a source of awe, respect and reverence. In this form of response to the world, the religious and secular versions of spirituality are very close to one another.

This takes us to the fifth strand of spirituality, namely, the cultivation of inner space. In religious spirituality this includes prayer, meditation and ritual often accompanied by meditative music.[17] There has been a great revival of interest in this kind of music – in particular, Gregorian chant. The exploration of inner space in secular contexts has prompted the development of meditative music with therapeutic purposes designed to provide moments of respite from the stress and pressure of life, for example, *The Chillout Album, Pan Pipe Moods*. In the educational context, the cultivation of inner space can take both religious and secular forms and classes devoted to meditation can take place as part of religious education or moral/pastoral education. This strand of spirituality is linked to the final dimension, that of absorption.

Absorption in an activity has both religious and secular aspects. Everyday life offers experience that can be described as spiritual in this sense. Aspects of this experience are to be found in any activity that we engage in for the pleasure of it, and not for an extrinsic purpose such as a reward. This is the kind of delight experienced by a person reading a poem or novel, watching a play, listening to a piece of music, or looking at a painting. We would describe this person as engrossed, absorbed, wrapped up or lost in what he or she is doing. In this situation we are talking of a very special identification between the individual and her/ his activity where the gap between the person and this activity is most reduced. I suspect that in these moments we come near to that loss of self involved in mystical experience. Responding to works of art can, therefore, offer rare moments in which some

17. I am grateful to my former student, Kathleen Kinsella, for her insights into this aspect of spirituality.

faint echoes of such experience are to be found. Whether we characterise this in religious or secular terms is really an individual matter.

Yet at the heart of the term 'spirituality' is a paradox. Both religious and non-religious people can be described as 'spiritual' and this always implies a very positive a moral evaluation of the individual. But when we speak of a religious person as being 'spiritual', it is a very high commendation of the quality of her or his religious engagement. In this usage being spiritual has a very strong religious sense and is entirely detached from any secular meaning.

Perhaps it is unrealistic to expect official documents to engage in such close analysis of terminology but it is necessary if we are to achieve clarity about aims. This analysis demonstrates that the notion of spirituality does not offer common ground between religious and non-religious views of life. And the term also occurs three times in the treatment of Religious Education, to which we now turn.

THE TREATMENT OF RELIGIOUS EDUCATION

Let us turn next to the treatment of Religious Education itself. The following is the full, final text on Religious Education and, for the sake of convenience, the aspects of the draft document are incorporated in italics.

In seeking to develop the full potential of the individual, the curriculum takes into account the child's affective, aesthetic, spiritual, moral and religious needs. The spiritual dimension is a fundamental aspect of individual experience, and its religious and cultural expression is an inextricable part of Irish culture and history. Religious education specifically enables the child to develop spiritual and moral values and to come to a knowledge of God.

Irish society recognises the right of the individual to choose the particular form of religious expression that reflects the spiritual aspirations and experience he or she seeks. It acknowledges, too, the importance of tolerance towards the practice, culture and life-style of a range of religious convictions and expressions, and aspires (draft: *strives*) to develop in children a tolerance and understanding towards the beliefs of others.

Education, generally, seeks to reflect and cater for a variety of religious conviction and acknowledges the right of parents to arrange for their children's education in a school whose religious ethos coincides with their own religious belief. It is the responsibility (draft: *duty*) of the school to provide a religious education that is consonant with its ethos and at the same time to be flexible in making alternative organisational arrangements for those who do not wish to avail of the particular religious education it offers. It is equally important that (draft: *in the course of a general engagement with the curriculum*) the beliefs and sensibilities of every child are respected.

Since the Department of Education and Science, in the context of the Education Act (1998), recognises (draft: *devolves*) the rights of (draft: *to*) the different Church authorities to design curricula in religious education at primary level and to supervise their teaching and implementation, a religious education curriculum is not included in these curriculum documents. [18]

The change from 'strives' to 'aspires' weakens the obligation on schools regarding the development of tolerance and the change from 'duty' to 'responsibility' could be understood as lessening the obligation on schools regarding the provision of Religious Education and regarding 'making alternative organisational arrangements' for the children of parents withdrawn from the classes in religion. Yet the change from 'devolves' to the weaker term 'recognises' attributes to the State a less active office in facilitating the promotion of religion. But the most significant

18. Department of Education and Science, *The Primary Curriculum: Introduction*, p. 58, and Pollack, 'New School Curriculum Leaves out God in Favour of Spiritual Dimension'.

change concerns the omission of the phrase '*in the course of a general engagement with the curriculum*'. This means that teachers do not have to avoid all reference to religion across the curriculum and consequently allows for integration between religion and other subjects. The *New Primary Curriculum* does not address the concerns of parents who object to this.

Before considering this matter, it is interesting to note that the study of religion does feature in the 1999 curriculum in spite of conceding the right to 'the different Church authorities to design curricula in religious education at primary level and to supervise their teaching and implementation'.[19] Religion is studied in the area of SESE, that is, Social Environmental and Scientific Education, which includes History and Geography.[20] The emphasis in these areas is of an inter-faith character that, as Patricia Kieran observes, contrasts with the 'vast majority of religious education teaching [which] occurs within a mono-faith perspective'.[21]

Kieran takes the History and Geography strands taught in third and fourth class as examples of the approach taken in SESE. The unit on 'Feasts and Festivals in the Past' introduces the children to the genesis and traditions of common festivals in Ireland and elsewhere and draws explicit attention to 'feasts and festivals celebrated by various members of the school and local community, including Christian, Hindu, Jewish, Muslim and other celebrations ...'[22] The strand on 'Story' aims to alert pupils to 'the lives of women, men and children from different social, cultural, ethnic and religious backgrounds...'[23] The aim of the

19. Department of Education and Science, *The Primary Curriculum: Introduction*, p. 58.
20. The scope of the cross-curricular study of religion has been perceptively and extensively analysed by Patricia Kieran 'Promoting Truth? Inter-Faith Education in Irish Catholic Primary Schools', Irish National Teachers' Organisation, *Teaching Religion in the Primary School: Issues and Challenges*, pp. 119-130. This paragraph is based on her chapter.
21. Ibid., p. 127.
22. Department of Education and Science, *Primary School Curriculum History* (Dublin: The Stationery Office, 1999). p. 44.
23. Ibid., p. 47.

Geography strand 'Human Environments' is to enable children to 'learn about and come to appreciate and respect the people and communities who live and work in the locality' and to make 'links with other people in other parts of Ireland and the world'.[24] A strand unit entitled 'People and Other Lands' examines the nature of religious belief in terms of the 'myths, stories, art, culture, clothes' of other peoples.[25]

The spirit of this aspect of religious education is non-catechetical and it is unlikely that secular parents would object to it. Furthermore, the INTO survey discloses a huge majority (over 86.1%) of those questioned were in favour of teaching about other religions and two thirds were in favour of incorporating this into the actual Religious Education programme.[26] Yet the problem remains of balancing the religious dimension of cultural initiation with respect for the wishes of parents who do not wish their children to encounter faith-based worldviews. Although the INTO has stressed the importance of having a 'clear policy' on how teachers should respond to meeting the 'spiritual needs of all of the children' in a school, this matter is not addressed at official level.[27] We turn our attention to it in the chapter that follows

24. Department of Education and Science, *Primary School Curriculum Geography* (Dublin: The Stationery Office, 1999). p. 54.

25. Ibid., p. 56.

26. Irish National Teachers' Organisation, *Teaching Religion in the Primary School,* p. 48.

27. Ibid., p. 50.

CHAPTER SIX

Schooling and the Demands of Diversity

An indication of the difficulty in Ireland of balancing the religious dimension of cultural initiation with respect for the wishes of parents who do not want their children to encounter faith worldviews is the failure, already noted, to establish the working party proposed in the 1995 White Paper on Education to make recommendations on the issue. By contrast, there is a multiplicity of committees and agencies addressing disadvantage and low achievement about which consensus is nearly total. It is hard to avoid the conclusion that the politicians and bureaucrats fight shy of contentious topics that give rise to genuine disagreement. What John Walshe wrote in 1991 remains true today: politicians try to avoid the 'risky issue of religion in schools'.[1] Although the working party was not established, the Education Act made definition of ethos a matter for individual schools. This means that over 90% of primary schools will remain confessional and overwhelmingly under the control of the Churches.

The religious worldview endorsed by over 90% of primary schools is bound to pervade their ethos, including their curriculum. Accordingly, it is not easy to see how a pupil could avoid the influence of religion without being withdrawn from a school's whole programme of education. Realistically, it would be impossible to ensure that the children are not exposed to the influence of religion through the school's ethos and within its curriculum. So, although the official requirement to integrate religion with other subjects ended in 1999, integration occurs in practice with the result that parents who do not wish their children to be

---

1. John Walshe, 'Minister Being Forced to Tackle Risky Issue of Religion in Schools', *The Irish Times*, 12 November, 1991, p.10.

exposed to religious influence cannot have these wishes realised in confessional schools.

This situation is not repugnant to the Irish Constitution. As noted in Chapter Three, the right not to attend religious instruction cannot protect a child 'from being influenced, to some degree, by the religious "ethos" of the school'.[2] Although any attempt at proselytism is explicitly ruled out and the right to withdraw from Religious Education is affirmed, school management is 'not obliged to change the general atmosphere of its school merely to accommodate a child of a different religious persuasion who wishes to attend that school'.[3]

It is important that judicial reasoning on educational issues be informed by appropriate philosophical and empirical research in the area but we must distinguish between legal and educational/moral grounds for decisions. It is not sufficient simply to invoke a constitutional provision, a law or even a judicial determination as if this ended all moral and philosophical discussion on an issue. In any case, although judicial determinations are binding in law, these determinations derive from judgements about the weight to be placed on different elements in a mosaic of principles. The judgement of the High and Supreme Courts in the chaplaincy case, for example, did not derive from insights derived from the heavens and could have been different.[4]

Is it therefore possible to reconcile liberal educational principles with respect for the beliefs and commitments of the children of parents who are not Catholics? Note here that, although I am speaking of parents, I am not persuaded that conferring all rights on parents rather than on children themselves is always in the best interests of these children. As is common elsewhere, however, the Irish legislation is framed in terms of parental wishes

2. Campaign to Separate Church and State Ltd and Jeremiah Noel Murphy v Minister for Education, the Attorney General, The Most Reverend Cathal Daly, The Most Reverend Desmond Connell, The Most Reverend Dermot Clifford and the Most Reverend Joseph Cassidy, *Irish Law Review Monthly*, 2 (1998), pp. 81-101, p. 101.
3. Ibid.
4. See John M. Kelly, *The Irish Constitution*, edited by G. Hogan and G. Whyte, fourth edition (Dublin: LexisNexis, 2003), paras. 7.8. 69-70, pp. 2057-8.

and it is not appropriate in this context to problematise the matter. As in areas of the United Kingdom, the solution of providing separate non-confessional schools in rural areas for the children of the small minority of non-believing parents is not economically realistic.[5] In any case, even if it were possible to establish separate schools to accommodate the children of parents who object to the ethos of the local school, it is questionable whether the educational interests of these children would be best served by such segregation.

CONTROL OF SCHOOLS

Before continuing, it is appropriate to make some brief comments about the control of schools, although, as I stated in the Introduction, this book is not about the patronage, control or management of schools.

I do not know if new schools of the future will come under the same kind of confessional patronage and management as the schools of today. In the light of information provided by the New Schools Advisory Committee concerning proposals for new schools in September 2005, there is, however, clear evidence of a striking trend towards the Educate Together model.[6] Also the survey conducted on behalf of the Department of Education and Science in summer 2004 indicates that the sample population is evenly divided on the desirability of providing separate schools that reflect that cultural or religious background of parents.[7] Furthermore, 61% of those surveyed believe that schools should not be denominational but should provide for the teaching of

5. A report in The Guardian Education Section considers the dilemma of such parents in the United Kingdom. See Karen Gold, 'Faith in Our Schools', *Guardian Education* (25 April 2000), pp. 2-3.

6. Of the proposed new schools, twelve are under the patronage of Educate Together, three are under Catholic patronage, three are Gaelscoileanna, and one is under the joint patronage of the Catholic and Church of Ireland bishops. See New Schools Advisory Committee, Public Consultation on Proposed New Primary Schools for September 2005 (Tullamore : Department of Education and Science, 2004).

7. See Thomas Kellaghan, Páid McGee, David Millar, Rachel Perkins, *Views of the Irish Public on Education: 2004 Survey* (Dublin: Educational Research Centre, 2004), pp. 14, 34. http://www.education.ie Accessed 15 November 2004.

religion and almost 50% believe that schools should not be denominational and that the teaching of religion should be provided outside of school hours.

We have seen in the Introduction to this volume how complex and nuanced are the terms used in respect of different kinds of school, and it is possible that respondents to the survey were not entirely clear about the meaning and implications of the terms used. In any event, it is a pity that they were not asked for their views about ecumenical schools.

These schools are beginning to emerge as an alternative to the traditional confessional and to the Educate Together models. Under joint Catholic/Church of Ireland patronage, the ethos of ecumenical schools differs from that in Educate Together schools. This ethos allows both for a thicker, more substantial and robust concept of the good than that of tolerance alone as well as a more salient profile assigned to Religious Education through its inclusion within the normal school day. Several schools under the auspices of *Foras Patrúnachta Scoileanna Lán Ghaeilge* have adopted ecumenical models of management and the dispute in Dunboyne over the teaching of religion should not discourage communities from applying the inter-faith model or from exploring other forms of school management.[8]

John Carr of the INTO has some interesting points to make about the notion of a 'community school' at primary level. In a suggestion that reflects the spirit of the Stanley Letter of 1831, Carr envisages the establishment of state schools that accommodate the teaching of religion to children of different faiths.[9] This,

8. There is a valuable account of the ecumenical ethos of Gaelscoil Chill Mhantain in a letter entitled 'Interdenominational Schools' by Siobhán Uí Mhaonaile in *The Irish Times*, 30 April 2002, p. 15. As noted in Chapter Three, this issue is discussed by Pádraig Hogan in 'Religion in Education and the Integrity of Teaching as a Practice: The Experience of Irish National Schools in Changing Times' in *Teaching Religion in the Primary School: Issues and Challenges*, Irish National Teachers' Organisation, (Dublin: Irish National Teachers' Organisation, 2003), pp. 69-71.

9. Irish National Teachers' Organisation, 'Open Forum' in *Teaching Religion in the Primary School: Issues and Challenges* (Dublin: Irish National Teachers' Organisation, 2003), pp. 95-6.

I should add, occurs at second level where Community Schools and Community Colleges have structures of management and control that reconcile the legitimate concerns of different educational partners. This approach may offer a fruitful model for the primary schools of the future.

A persuasive case has been made that at second-level the spirit of a Christian education finds authentic expression in the schools in the Community sector.[10] As Joe Dunne put it in 1991 with regard to the situation at primary level, Catholics need to ask whether making a 'distinctive contribution' to a 'school for the whole community', a contribution that has genuine purchase in the life of the school, 'may not be a better choice than holding out for a school of their own'.[11] Indeed, in her study of Irish Catholicism since 1950, Louise Fuller notes the unease of 'many religious' with the Church's preoccupation with 'controlling and managing the system'.[12] These religious question whether 'Catholic management and control equated with a Catholic ethos' and suggest the importance of communicating the Christian vision at the 'much deeper level' of personal witness.[13]

RESPECTING BELIEFS AND SENSIBILITIES

Whatever about the future, let us address the situation as it exists in the vast majority of primary schools because, as Pádraig Hogan notes, we are not starting with a 'clean slate'.[14] In the light of government policy, can anything more be done to vindicate the wishes of non-religious parents? By exploring what might be meant in the White Paper by the notion of 'good practice' in responding to the children of these parents, elements of an approach might be identified. In identifying these, I propose to

10. See James Norman, *Ethos and Education* (New York: Peter Lang, 2003).

11. Joseph Dunne, 'The Catholic School and Civil Society: Exploring the Tensions', in *The Catholic School in Contemporary Society*, Conference of Major Religious Superiors (Dublin: Conference of Major Religious Superiors, 1991), pp.18-46, p. 44.

12. Louise Fuller, *Irish Catholicism Since 1950: The Undoing of a Culture* (Dublin: Gill and Macmillan, 2004), p. 174 .

13. Ibid., p. 173.

14. See Irish National Teachers' Organisation, 'Open Forum' in *Teaching Religion in the Primary School: Issues and Challenges*, p. 97.

develop the approach adopted in some significant judicial determinations that are relevant to the issue.

The first is a judgement of the European Court of Human Rights in a case taken by Danish parents against the integration of sex education into the general school curriculum. According to the judgement, the communication of knowledge of an indirectly religious or philosophical character within schools could not be prohibited 'for otherwise all institutionalised teaching would run the risk of proving impracticable'.[15] Many school subjects have

> to a greater or lesser extent, some philosophical complexion or implications. The same is true of religious affinities if one remembers the existence of religions forming a very broad dogmatic and moral entity which has or may have answers to every question of a philosophical, cosmological or moral nature.[16]

But the 'information or knowledge included in the curriculum' must be

> conveyed in an objective, critical and pluralistic manner. The State is forbidden to pursue an aim of indoctrination that might be considered as not respecting parents' religious and philosophical convictions. This is the limit that must not be exceeded.[17]

Furthermore, teachers must ensure that 'parents' religious and philosophical convictions are not disregarded ... by carelessness, lack of judgement or misplaced proselytism'.[18] In this comment we find an echo of the injunction in the Stanley Letter of 1831 to avoid 'even the suspicion of proselytism'[19] and that the

15. Kjeldsen, Busk, Madsen and Pedersen v. Denmark, European Human Rights Reports, Series A, No. 23 (1976), pp. 711-736.

16. Ibid.

17. Ibid., p. 731.

18. Ibid. p 732.

19. See Áine Hyland and Kenneth Milne, eds., Irish Educational Documents, Vol. 1 (Dublin: The Church of Ireland College of Education, 1987), pp. 99 and 100.

'most scrupulous care should be taken not to interfere with the peculiar tenets of any description of Christian pupils'.[19]

The second case to be examined is the judgement of the Federal Constitutional Court of Germany in an action0 taken against the display of crucifixes in the publicly-funded schools of Bavaria. The Court was concerned to balance a tension addressed in this volume in the Irish context. This is the tension between, on the one hand, the historical salience of Christianity in German culture and, on the other hand, respect for diversity, in particular, the freedom 'due to all parents and pupils equally, not just the Christian ones'.[20]

Appeal to the 'majority principle' was found to be inappropriate because the 'fundamental right to religious freedom specifically is aimed in a special degree at protecting minorities'.[21] The Court confirmed that German law permits the State to support the promotion of religious beliefs as long as the practices concerned are 'voluntary and allow the other-minded acceptable, non-discriminatory possibilities of avoiding them', and as long as this support is 'associated with only the indispensable minimum of elements of compulsion'.[22]

But it found that the presence of the crucifix was inconsistent with these conditions and with respect for freedom of religion. According to the judgment, the crucifix is not merely a 'token of the Western cultural tradition' but rather a symbol of 'the essential core of the conviction of the Christian faith, which has undoubtedly shaped the Western world in particular in many ways but is certainly not shared by all members of society, and is indeed rejected by many'.[23]

---

20. The relevant section of the judgement can be found in an English translation in Katarina Tomasevski, *Human Rights in Education as a Prerequisite for Human Rights Education: Right to Education Primer No. 4* (Gotenburg, Swedish International Development Cooperation Agency, 2001), p. 36-7, p. 37. http://www.right-to-education.org Accessed 30 March 2004.

21. Ibid.

22. Ibid.

23. Ibid.

GOOD PRACTICE: THE INSTITUTIONAL LEVEL

The relevant features of these judgements are the avoidance of indoctrination and the minimising of exposure to religion especially through the availability of appropriate arrangements for avoiding it. Consistent with these judgements, the notion of 'good practice' can be said to have two aspects, institutional and individual. On the institutional level, confessional schools must be hospitable to the development of autonomy in young people both in general and in respect of religious belief in particular.

Here it is possible to draw a distinction between open and closed confessional schools. Open confessional schools are hospitable to the promotion of such autonomy, whereas certain confessional schools (arguably, all fundamentalist schools whether Christian, Jewish, Muslim or Hindu) do not aspire to the cultivation of intellectual autonomy at all. These are best described as closed confessional schools.

Note, however, that closed secular or non-confessional schools which exclude any encounter with religion belief from the school can also be said to set limits to the autonomous development of children in as far as this approach is inhospitable to the possibility of coming to embrace religious commitment.

In Ireland, confessional primary schools must be prepared to accommodate children of non-believing parents or of parents with beliefs different from those of the school. Under the Irish Constitution, because primary education is compulsory, schools can be obliged to accept any child within their catchment area, irrespective of the beliefs of the parents, if there is no school whose ethos is acceptable to the parents in question. As we saw in Chapter Three, refusal to accept a pupil is permissible only where 'it is proved that the refusal is essential to maintain the ethos of the school … '[24]

In any case, although the fundamental disagreement between theistic and non-theistic worldviews should not be minimised, there are elements of some common ground between believer

24. Government of Ireland, Equal Status Act 2000 (Dublin: The Stationery Office, 2000), Section 7 (3) (C).

and non-believer with regard to moral values.

The Norwegian approach captures the possibility of shared ground between believer and non-believer with regard to moral values in its recommendations that 'Biblical similes' as well as 'illustrations from other religions, from history, fiction, biography, and from legends, parables, myths and fables' be used as part of moral education.[25] It is true that there is a relationship between the values that are promoted in schools hospitable to a Christian religious ethos and moral values in general. Many of the central moral values promoted in such schools are also acceptable to non-believers. Generosity, concern for others and consideration of their interests, willingness to share and to co-operate, courage and steadfastness are among the values which inform a religious ethos and which would be perfectly acceptable to believer and non-believer alike. The ideals of human conduct enshrined in such parables as the Good Samaritan and the Prodigal Son and in the injunctions in the Sermon on the Mount form part of the moral capital of Western civilisation.

Faith schools derive their identity from a vision of life that goes 'beyond utility',[26] beyond what, in his poem 'The World Is Too Much with Us', Wordsworth describes as 'getting and spending'. Concern with the consumer orientation of education today has become tiresomely commonplace in contemporary social commentary. I have little patience with moralising claims about a contemporary 'ethic of individual consumption' or about an 'individualist, competitive, acquisitive culture' that appear to find that the human beings have become dramatically more selfish and greedy over the generations.

Moreover, I am far from persuaded by the commonly canvassed suggestion[27] that young people today are more trivial and

25. The Royal Ministry of Education, Research and Church Affairs, *Core Curriculum for Primary, Secondary and Adult Education in Norway* (Oslo: National Centre for Educational Resources, 1997), p. 9.

26. Mary McCarthy, *Memories of a Catholic Girlhood* (Harmondsworth, London: Penguin, 1967), p. 26.

27. See, for example, the comments in Régis Debray, *L'Enseignement du Fait Religieux dans L'École Laïque* (Paris: Editions Odile Jacob, 2002), pp. 17-8.

present-oriented than previous generations. It is not easy to provide evidence regarding the moral and civic propensities of human beings and impossible to generate this retrospectively, but we should be wary of romanticising the past and assuming that things were different then. Faith schools have, however, always very explicitly pointed young people to the essential values and purposes of human life and introduced them to a quality of life which lies beyond the mere fact of living.[28] Much within this moral and civic outreach is consistent with the remit of any educational institution.

I do not believe that a Catholic education has a monopoly over civic and moral virtue, and I think that it is misguided to arrogate to Catholic schools alone concern with the welfare of others. In this country, the Vocational Education sector has a long and distinguished record in the education of the poor. The altruistic orientation that is a feature of faith-inspired schools can there-fore be shared with those who do not necessarily share the faith of the school community.

This takes us to a final and sensitive aspect of the institutional dimension of 'good practice'. This concerns the response of the school to teachers who find themselves unable to teach religion in a confessional context. My experience leads me to have confidence that school authorities will respond sympathetically to the plight of such teachers. After all, teachers in Ireland, as Andrew McGrady puts it, 'make a decision to teach', rather than making the 'decision to teach within a school which defines itself as an "ecclesial community".'[29] For example, among the teachers who responded to the recent INTO survey, the figure for those who 'teach religion willingly' is 61.2%.[30]

28. Here I have slightly adapted a sentence from A.N. Whitehead, *Religion in the Making* (Cambridge: Cambridge University Press, 1926), p. 80.

29. Andrew G. McGrady, 'The Religious Dimension of Education in Irish Second Level Schools at the Start of the Third Millennium', *REA/Religion, Education and the Arts*, vol. 4 (2003), pp. 53-87, p. 83. The point is made in connection with second-level schools but also applies at primary level.

30. Irish National Teachers' Organisation, *Teaching Religion in the Primary School Issues and Challenges*, p. 48.

Yet the survey also indicates that the number who actually wish to opt out of teaching religion is small – some 10% of those who responded to survey.[31] But for these teachers I am impressed by Joe Dunne's suggestion that the Catholic school 'enlarge its self-understanding so that it could welcome – I say welcome not just "tolerate" – a teacher who dissents from the Catholic faith but who shows respect for the religious beliefs and practices in the school'.[32] Although such a teacher would not be expected to adopt a catechetical role, Dunne suggests that a school might 'find a way of honouring her or his conscientiously held convictions and, should she or he so wish, allow the latter explicitly to enrich the educational milieu of the school'.[33] What Paul Rowe argues in respect of Educate Together schools represents appropriate practice for any school. Teachers should 'not have to teach as religious truths beliefs that they may not themselves hold'.[34]

Let us turn next to an exploration of the individual aspect of the notion of 'good practice'.

GOOD PRACTICE: THE INDIVIDUAL LEVEL

Whether it is possible or appropriate to provide detail and elaboration on the individual aspect of the notion beyond the identification of general conditions is debatable. One general condition that will certainly apply is the requirement of teachers to exercise the utmost tact in their response to the children of non-believing parents. What is necessary here is the human and moral sensitivity that is a feature of all good teaching. Pádraig Hogan has described this attitude as respecting the 'integrity of teaching as a practice'.[35] This sensitivity and this respect will go beyond the admonition to be 'careful, in presence of children of

31. Ibid., pp. 47-8. 10% is a round figure of teachers in different categories in the survey. Striking is the reluctance of almost 40% to facilitate a colleague who had opted out. See ibid., p. 51
32. Dunne, 'The Catholic School and Civil Society: Exploring the Tensions', p. 45.
33. Ibid.
34. Paul Rowe, 'Inclusive Schools Need More Support', *The Irish Times*, 4 October 2004, p. 14.
35. Pádraig Hogan, 'Religion in Education and the Integrity of Teaching as

different religious beliefs, not to touch on matters of contro-versy',[36] the phrase that was deleted from the *Rules for National Schools* in 1965.

The sensitivity and respect in question will involve, for exam-ple, the avoidance of offensive or stigmatising comments about non-believers. Karen Gold reports the case of the son of British Humanist Association member, Julie Norris, being poked and disparaged by his teacher for not putting his hands together and praying with his eyes closed.[37] A parent in Alvey's book gives an example of an eight-year-old boy responding to a question from a teacher (not his regular teacher) about why he did not do religion by saying that he did not believe in God. The teacher grabbed the child's ruler, broke it in two, placed the two parts together in the shape of a cross and asked him what it was.[38] These actions are obviously unacceptable.

Another expression of pedagogic tact is the presentation of material that integrates religion with other subjects in a manner that avoids 'even the suspicion of proselytism'.[39]

Openness

This tact involves an openness on the part of the individual teacher reflecting the openness at the institutional level. This will demand a willingness to listen to other voices in the classroom in Religious Education or during other lessons. Two literary texts illustrate the nature of this tact and openness.

A characterisation of tact is to be found in Chinua Achebe's novel, *Things Fall Apart*. The Christian missionary, Mr Brown, 'spent long hours'[40] with the village chief discussing religion.

a Practice: The Experience of Irish National Schools in Changing Times in *Teaching Religion in the Primary School: Issues and Challenges*, Irish National Teach-ers' Organisation, (Dublin: Irish National Teachers' Organisation, 2003), pp.119-130.

36. See Áine Hyland and Kenneth Milne, eds., *Irish Educational Documents*, Vol II (Dublin: The Church of Ireland College of Education, 1992), pp. 106, 135.

37. Gold, 'Faith in Our Schools' , *Guardian Education*, p. 3.

38. David Alvey, *Irish Education: The Case for Secular Reform* (Dublin/Belfast: Church and State Books/Athol Books, 1991), p. 15

39. See Hyland and Milne, eds., *Irish Educational Documents*, Vol. 1, pp. 99.

40. Chinua Achebe, *Things Fall Apart* (London: Heinemann,1986), p. 128.

Although neither 'succeeded in converting the other', they both 'learnt more about their different beliefs'[41] as a result of their willingness to listen to one another with openness and respect.

Even more striking is the account of the experience of openness to encountering other worldviews to be found in James Cowan's novel, *A Mapmaker's Dream*. The narrator, a sixteenth century monk, Fra Maura, is translating a Turkish text and finds himself

> confronted with another man's view of the world and ... in contact with perceptions entirely different from my own. The world as Hadji Ahmed saw it was a potpourri of facts slanted toward the glorification of Allah and the supremacy of Sulieman as the padishah of the Ottomans.[42]

Fra Maura does not know what to think and wonders if the author is an 'imposter' or else if he enjoyed access to knowledge closed to one brought up in Europe. The more he translated, the more he 'began to believe that neither of us had a hegemony over truth'.[43] I am not persuaded that we have to embrace such relativism about truth but we do need to exercise openness towards the beliefs of others.

The parent quoted by Alvey gives an example of another teacher who, although himself very religious, was sympathetic to her son's position. This teacher reproved the other boys for attempting to stigmatise the child for his atheism and told them that they were lucky to have a classmate who had different beliefs.[44] The Catholic Church itself has an open attitude towards the presence in Catholic schools of non-Catholic pupils, as well as an awareness of the existence in these schools of pupils who are non-believers.[45] Indeed, common sense suggests that, if young

41. Ibid.
42. James Cowan, A *Mapmaker's Dream* (New York: Warners Books, 1986), p. 39.
43. Ibid.
44. Alvey, *Irish Education: The Case for Secular Reform*, p. 16.
45. Congregation for Catholic Education, *The Religious Dimension of Education in a Catholic School: Guidelines for Reflection and Renewal* (London: Catholic Truth Society, 1988), pp. 5 and 57-8.

people do not enjoy opportunities for interaction with those who differ from them in their childhood years, they will at the very least find it more difficult to understand and to relate to such individuals as adults.

There are indeed indications that pedagogic tact is already exercised in practice. For example, some years ago, Jackie Bourke, a journalist from *The Irish Times,* found that increasingly faith schools are reaching out to children of different faith backgrounds and of none.

Here are the comments of the teacher of a sixth class where pupils are making their Confirmation regarding the accommodation of children who are not. The latter 'join in class discussion' where pupils 'talk about different beliefs, and why some children are not making their confirmation'.[46] 'The important thing', remarks the teacher, 'is to respect each child's individuality'.[47]

At the institutional level, this respect is also given practical expression through the provision in the school of a non-confessional meditation room.

These practices are consistent with the spirit of the response by the late Christina Murphy in 1995 to parents who were concerned about having to send their children to a confessional school. She gave several reasons for advising non-religious parents to allow their children to attend religion class in the local school and it is worth rehearsing these briefly. She drew attention to the risk of stigmatising by peers and consequent bullying if the child is withdrawn from RE class. She made the point canvassed in this book about the importance of coming to an understanding of religion because it is a historically significant aspect of Irish culture.[48] Murphy also suggested that the negative views of some parents may be based on their own experiences of the stern

46. Jackie Bourke, 'Ye of Little Faith', *The Irish Times; Education and Living Supplement,* 3 February 1998, p. 5.

47. Ibid.

48. Christina Murphy, 'Question and Answer', *The Irish Time: Education and Living Supplement,* 29 September 1995, p. 9.

régimes of earlier times. Issues to do with ownership and control of schools that prompt public discussion and disagreement may have little enough impact, she felt, on everyday life in schools.[49]

What about Indoctrination?

But, readers may wonder, what about the danger of indoctrination both in the course of the school curriculum generally or especially during Religious Education, which, in primary schools, is catechetical in nature? I appreciate that the fear of indoctrination is not the only concern of parents who do not wish their children to undergo a confessional Religious Education programme, even if it is 'very broad and very enlightened'.[50] But I do think that it is worth drawing attention to the fact that fear of indoctrination is generally unfounded. Christina Murphy expressed doubts about its prevalence, observing that she had 'known agnostics and atheists who have sent their kids to the local national school, they weren't indoctrinated and they ended up with somewhat similar views to their parents'.[51] Indeed, recent years have witnessed even more exciting developments in this area. As Pádraig Hogan puts it with characteristic eloquence, there has been an 'historic shift – from a custodial conception of Christianity which has been traditional in more countries than Ireland, to one of an unforced and festive fellowship'.[52]

The findings of French researcher, Jean-Paul Willaime, following a review of confessional schooling in Germany, confirm a trend that will not surprise many close to the reality of school life in Ireland. He found that confessionalism at the institutional level does not necessarily translate into strong confessionalism in practice during Religious Education lessons. Teachers have to take into account the mindsets of children which can vary greatly due to a lack of homogeneous religious backgrounds even

49. Christina Murphy, 'Q and A/Question and Answer', *The Irish Times: Education and Living Supplement*, 9 May 1995, p. 9.

50. Murphy, 'Question and Answer', *The Irish Times: Education and Living Supplement*, 29 September 1995, p. 9.

51. Ibid.

52. Pádraig Hogan, 'Religion in Education and the Integrity of Teaching as a Practice: The Experience of Irish National Schools in Changing Times', p. 68.

among those whose parents have the same religion.[53] This leads Nicolas Truong to conclude that there is a growing convergence between the profile of religion in the secular schools of France and the confessional equivalents elsewhere. In the former an attempt is being made to communicate the religious dimension of culture and in the latter an attempt to situate religion in a broader cultural context.[54]

In any case, I have always been rather sceptical of claims regarding the susceptibility of young people to indoctrination. Both religious believers and secularists do well never to underestimate the robust resistance of young people to the proselytising designs of adults.

There is a memorable scene is Tessa de Loo's popular novel, *The Twins*, which captures this resistance very well. Lotte, one of the eponymous twins, is sent to a Calvinist school in Holland because she cannot be accommodated in the state school. Having had a non-religious upbringing at home, she is intrigued by what she is learning from her teacher of religion. By contrast, her peers have no interest whatever in the subject, having been 'brought up on religion like a daily dose of cod liver oil'.[55] Lotte gets the highest marks in the class in Religious Education but her knowledge does not encourage her to make the transition to religious commitment. What the school principal invites her to accept as 'profound truth', Lotte thinks of as being of the same status as the story of Snow White and belief in Santa Claus.[56]

My intuition is that opponents of formative education *in* religion (although in France we find objections even to the study *of* religion) seriously exaggerate the susceptibility of young people to indoctrination in this area. Having supervised hundreds of lessons in Religious Education, my conviction is that indoctrinatory designs are not only morally and educationally

53. I have translated and paraphrased Willaime's comments from an article by Nicolas Truong, *Enseigner les Religions: Chassé-Croisé Européen, Le Monde de L'Éducation*, no. 306 (septembre 2002), pp. 76-8, p. 78.

54. Ibid.

55. Tessa de Loo, *The Twins* (London: Arcadia, 2001), p. 74.

56. Ibid., p. 75-6.

reprehensible but that their manipulative intent is detected and rejected by the alert questioning of young minds whose common sense and intellectual independence never cease to impress me.

This perception has led me for a long time now to question the rights of parents either, on the one hand, to withhold their children from, or, on the other hand, to insist on their participation in, religion class. The primacy given to parents' rights does not do justice to the capacity of young people themselves to make these decisions for themselves, especially at senior cycle at second level. It is both futile and educationally reprehensible to attempt to subvert young people's capacity for what John Hewitt calls 'the stubborn habit of unfettered thought'.[57] Respecting the capacity for independent thought does not require that teachers embrace neutrality, the pursuit of which, in any case is misguided.[58]

Neutrality and Teaching

The notion that a teacher or a programme of study can be neutral and avoid the promotion of a particular viewpoint needs further examination on several grounds. In the first place, a culture itself may be imbued with a 'viewpoint'. In Ireland, as in other countries, it is just not possible to avoid allowing young people encounter religious views in the course of their schooling. Chapter One showed that cultural initiation can carry a significant religious loading in Ireland (and elsewhere) and this is expressed in the language, literature, history and place names of the country.

Secondly, the whole notion of the neutral teacher is highly questionable. In particular, the teaching of literature subverts the aspiration to the kind of detachment from the passion of lived human experience implied by neutrality. Let me develop here some points raised in the final section of Chapter Four.

57. From his poem 'The Dilemma' in Patricia Craig, ed., *The Oxford Book of Ireland* (Oxford: Oxford University Press, 1999), p. 300.

58. The difficulties in defending the notion of neutrality in education are perceptively explored by Signe Sandsmark in *Is World View Neutral Education Possible and Desirable?* (Carlisle: Paternoster Press, 2000).

Again I refer to the work of Denis Donoghue who captures this aspect of my argument very well. Part of the purpose and pleasure of reading literature involves 'a going out from oneself toward other lives, other forms of life, past, present, and perhaps future'.[59] Reading is therefore connected 'to sympathy, fellowship, the spirituality and morality of being human'.[60] Poet Michael Longley shows how this conception of reading takes on life in the classroom. One aim of the good teacher of poetry, as he puts it, is to explain to his pupils what a poem is 'doing to him, the teacher, spiritually, emotionally and intellectually'.[61]

Some metaphors that I drew upon in Chapter Four are again relevant here. Azar Nafisi describes learning to read literature in terms of learning to 'inhale' different experiences and of learning to 'feel like a stranger in your own home' that is, becoming unsettled with regard to dearly held beliefs.[62] Brendan Kennelly argues that poems 'that work get to the root of your position, they insist on becoming central to your life and may even change it'.[63] Such poetry 'reads you' in the sense that it 'really forces you to look at yourself' operating like a 'time bomb in the guts of complacency'.[64] To invoke once more the words of Harold Bloom and Samuel Johnson, literature can challenge us 'to weigh and consider' what we read in respect of how to make sense of the world and even to acquire knowledge of 'not just of self and others, but of the way things are'.[65] This means that students have

59. Denis Donoghue, *The Practice of Reading* (New Haven and London: Yale University Press, 1998), p. 73.

60. Ibid.

61. This extract from an interview with Michael Longley can be found in Siobhán McSweeney, 'The Poets' Picture of Education', *The Crane Bag*, vol. 7, no. (1983), pp. 134-142, p. 139.

62. Azar Nafisi, *Reading Lolita in Tehran: A Memoir in Books* (London and New York: Fourth Estate, 2004), pp. 111 and 94.

63. This quotation is taken from part of an interview with Brendan Kennelly in Siobhán McSweeney, 'The Poets' Picture of Education', *The Crane Bag*, vol. 7, no. (1983), pp. 134-142, p. 140.

64. These quotations from Kennelly are taken from Daniel Murphy, *Education and the Arts* (Dublin: School of Education, Trinity College, Dublin, 1987), p. 54.

65. Harold Bloom, *How to Read and Why* (London: Fourth Estate, 2001), pp. 21, 29. The first quotation is taken by Bloom from Johnson and the second is Bloom's own.

to be enabled to engage critically with their own beliefs and commitments in the process of encountering those expressed in literature. In this way, the study of some literary texts will involve the facilitation on the part of learners of an honest, personalised engagement with their own and other worldviews.

The classroom cannot therefore be an arena purged of contamination from the 'breathing human passion'[66] generated by beliefs and commitments. To return to the point made at the end of Chapter Four, in provoking encounters with worldviews, the teaching of literature subverts both the aspiration to neutrality as well as to moral and ideological protectionism.

In the third place, there are issues concerning the relationship between the nature of knowledge and the aspiration to be neutral. Here we need to note a distinction between two attitudes. The first is that we cannot provide answers on certain questions, for example, whether God exists, or whether there is an afterlife. According to this argument, it is impossible in principle to reach any conclusion regarding such issues. This is not really neutrality; it is agnosticism. According to the second version of neutrality, these issues are highly contested and will always give rise to disagreement between people. Consequently, as is the policy in France and the United States, consideration of these issues should be excluded from the school because of its status as a neutral public or civic space.

The problem with the form of neutrality that excludes study of religion and other worldviews from schools is that it implies that one worldview is good as another. Choice of worldview may become represented as a matter of opinion. Young people can therefore get the impression that there is no ultimate criterion of truth or even of relative compellability that can be invoked in choosing between different worldviews. This suggests to them that the beliefs of eccentric cults have the same status as the beliefs of the great world religions or of atheism. This is not neutrality; it is relativism gone wild.

66. I take this phrase from line 28 of 'Ode on a Grecian Urn' by John Keats.

The version of neutrality that excludes the study of religion from the public school system has, in the United States, been criticised as a dereliction of duty on the part of educational authorities on the grounds that it prevents the scrutiny of religious truth claims within the classroom. Young people therefore come to form their views without appropriate pedagogic guidance.[67] In the USA it seems to me that the failure to accommodate the study of religion in school has led to the domination, if not indeed colonisation, of religious discourse in the public sphere by the voices of unreasoning, sanctimonious righteousness.

Yet it is due to the inevitability of engagement with religious truth-claims that the secularist (*läic*) system in France excludes any kind of study of religion from schools. The French approach is based on the view that just as students cannot study the history of philosophy without engaging in philosophical reasoning, they cannot study religion without thinking seriously about religious matters. But without engaging with the character of religious claims to truth, young people may dismiss religion entirely or else uncritically adopt views that they have inherited or that they encounter outside of the school.

The Educate Together sector in Ireland is to be commended for ensuring that children enjoy the opportunity to engage in the study of religion under the guidance of their teachers. In a piece in *The Irish Times* on *Learn Together: An Ethical Education Curriculum for Educate Together Schools,* Paul Rowe, chief executive of the organisation, writes that the teacher acts as a 'guide' in encouraging pupils to 'explore, evaluate and assess different viewpoints in an atmosphere of respect'.[68] In helping pupils to 'evaluate and assess different viewpoints', teachers cannot be neutral on religious matters because it will be part of every teacher's remit to

67. See the discussion of the current debate in Suzanne Rosenblith and Scott Priestman, 'Problematizing Religious Truth: Implications for Public Education', *Educational Theory,* vol. 54, no. 4 (2004), pp. 365-80.

68. Rowe, 'Inclusive Schools Need More Support', *The Irish Times,* 4 October 2004, p. 14.

enable learners to respect the force of better arguments. Reference to evaluation and assessment assumes the existence of criteria of truth and plausibility with regard to the claims of different religions. To be sure, conclusive proof cannot be provided in respect of the claims of faith but there exist nonetheless degrees of reasonableness in the area. No teacher can be neutral about the force of better arguments in respect of claims to reasonableness.

In the light of these arguments about the limits of neutrality, what is to be said regarding the expressions by teachers of their own viewpoints in the classroom? Is it educationally or pedagogically appropriate for a teacher to refuse to answer direct questions about her or his own religious view? I am referring here to such fundamental questions as, for example, whether God exists, whether Jesus was divine, or whether there is an afterlife. Obviously it is impossible to conceive of anyone, let alone a teacher, being without an opinion concerning these and other great questions about life and its purposes. I do not think that answers to these questions have to be prohibited in the classroom because of fears of partisanship on the part of teachers.

There is a parallel in the teaching of history. I am not persuaded that teachers of history, any more than teachers of literature, morality or religion, can be neutral; but this does not mean that they have to be partisan. We do have to choose between neutrality and partisanship. In France, the search for an unattainable neutrality has led to extravagant efforts to avoid any reference to personal beliefs. Teachers are warned to avoid what has been referred to as 'the trap of proselytism or of militant atheism' that may be the result of an inadvertent remark.[69] This fear could lead to a paralysing reticence on the part of teachers. The approach I propose is for teachers to be non-defensive, honest and prepared to entertain questions about their beliefs.

69. These remarks from a college lecturer are quoted in Luc Cédelle, '*Parler Religion en Toute Laïcité*', *Le Monde de L'Éducation*, no. 321 (janvier 2004), pp. 30-32, p. 32. The translation of the quoted remarks is mine.

Obviously teachers have to be sensitive and exercise pedagogic tact in doing so. The injunctions in the Stanley letter still
have currency here. These are the 'most scrupulous care should
be taken not to interfere with the peculiar tenets of any description of Christian pupils' and to avoid 'even the suspicion of
proselytism'.[70] The requirement of teachers in Community
Schools, referred to in Chapter Three, is also relevant. 'A teacher
shall not advertently and consistently seek to undermine the
religious belief or practice of any pupil in the school.'[71] This
seems to me to be a reasonable requirement of any teacher in any
school in respect of any worldview conscientiously held by any
pupil. Having had the privilege of visiting many schools on a
professional basis and of working with many teachers, indeed
from what I observe as a parent, I have confidence in the
common sense, sensitivity and pedagogic tact of teachers.

IN SEARCH OF BALANCE

The right of teachers to give expression to a religious view of
life is defensible as long as this expression subscribes to the
conditions of pedagogic tact. It is hardly realistic to expect that
teachers can do more to respect the wishes of non-believing
parents. In any case, encountering expressions of religious
beliefs in school allows the children of non-religious parents
some access to a worldview that could remain closed to them.
This can be only to the benefit of their general education.
Indeed, although no one would wish to deny parents their right
to withdraw their children from Religious Education, the exercise of this right does ignore any possible right which young
people might be said to have to an education in religion in any
formative sense.

Issues concerning rights are complex, yet there is a need to
consider the appropriate balance between the rights of parents,

70. See Hyland and Milne, eds., *Irish Educational Documents*, Vol. 1, pp. 100 and
99.

71. Association of Community Schools, Model Lease for Community Schools
(Dublin: Association of Community Schools, 1992), Section 7 D, p. 22.

the rights of children and the duty of educators to ensure that the education of young people in their charge is as comprehensive as possible regarding the good in human life. If the children of non-believing parents are not exposed to religion in school, they may never encounter religion as a significant source of meaning in human life. This is one reason why Religious Education should be incorporated within the general curriculum, although parents should retain the right to withdraw their children from it. I do not think that it is enough simply to allow parents to organise religion lessons outside school hours. This makes religion appear as peripheral or, at least, non-mainstream, in the education of young people. Indeed, even in France, the home of secular, civic neutrality (*laïcité*) in schooling, two regions, Alsace and Moselle, enjoy an historic right to have optional confessional Religious Education included in the school day as part of publicly-funded educational provision.

To return to the Irish context, there is much to be said for the wisdom of the vast majority of teachers on the issue. Of the teachers who responded to the recent INTO survey, 80.1% believe that RE should be taught during normal school hours and, as noted in Chapter Five, 86.1% believe that children should be taught about other religions, while two thirds think that this should take place during RE class.[72]

I am impressed by these views of the professionals in the area, although the evidence mentioned earlier in this chapter suggests that the general population may not share them to the same extent. But experience has taught me is that it is not very difficult to expel religion from people's lives. A principal in a Community School some time ago said to me: 'One of the reasons we like to encourage young people to go to religion class, and in fact to attend school liturgies, is that some do not encounter religious practice outside of the school'. The only exposure these young people will get to religion as a good in human life is therefore in school.

72. Irish National Teachers' Organisation, *Teaching Religion in the Primary School: Issues and Challenges*, p. 48.

There is a moment in the autobiography of Aminatta Forna where the absence of any Religious Education in a child's life is memorably communicated. Culturally a Muslim, Forna had been brought up in no religion at all. The incident occurs in Sierra Leone when she comes across her grandfather at prayer. She is confused about how to respond but the idea 'lodged' in her head that she too should be praying.

> So I knelt behind him, copying all his movements with no earthly idea what it all meant. Halfway through I began to feel foolish and decided to extricate myself, but that posed a new difficulty: to sidle away midway through prayers might seem sinful; at the same time I worried my grandfather might think I was making fun of him. I couldn't make the decision, so I went on, standing, kneeling and bowing for what seemed like eternity.[73]

The grandfather concluded his prayers without acknowledging her presence but she got the impression that he understood 'better than I, the struggle that had played out in my young mind'.[74] This incident captures the disablement that absence of any education in religion can engender.

To be sure, such illiteracy with regard to religion can be addressed by means of an age-appropriate course in religious studies or sociology of religion. Such courses are fine as far they go, but their existence does not imply that we must replace confessionally-specific Religious Education with this kind of study of religion as a phenomenon. Respect for liberal principles does not preclude initiating children into a specific religion. It is hard to see how we can actually teach religion in a serious sense without such initiation, any more than we can teach sport without actually teaching children to play a specific game or activity, or to teach languages without teaching a particular language.

73. Aminatta Forna, *The Devil that Danced on the Water* (London: Flamingo, 2003), p. 52.
74. Ibid., p. 53.

Jim Mackenzie makes this point by drawing on the words of George Santayana: 'The attempt to speak without speaking any particular language is not more hopeless than the attempt to have a religion that shall be no religion in particular'.[75]

This is why I question whether it is realistic to expect that a programme of Religious Education that is not denominationally-specific can initiate young people into the lived and living experience of a religious tradition. Religious Education from a faith perspective, where conducted with tact and honesty, is perfectly compatible with respect for diversity. Given that there exists no view from nowhere, the basis for 'genuine open and mutually respectful dialogue with other faiths', is, as David Carr argues with some metaphorical force, most appropriately 'nurtured in the soil of proper intellectual engagement with the grammar of some particular faith'.[76]

In conclusion, I wish to comment on the possible objection that subscription to the conditions of pedagogic tact will compromise the integrity of Religious Education. I would point out that the exercise of this tact does not mean that teachers have to tolerate obstructionism from children of parents with different beliefs. But this is something that applies across the curriculum. For example, pupils may have strong views about republicanism but the tiresome rehearsal of these views cannot be allowed to disrupt the normal teaching of history. But I repeat the point that the pedagogic tact of which I write is no more than the human and moral sensitivity that is a feature of all good teaching. In dealing with children, candour and non-defensive honesty are what are required – on moral and educational and practical grounds. In observing these values and demonstrating these

75. Jim Mackenzie, 'David Carr on Religious Knowledge and Spiritual Education', *Journal of Philosophy of Education*, vol. 32, no. 3 (November 1998), pp. 409-27, p. 421. The quotation from Santayana is taken from George Santayana, *The Life of Reason*, one volume edition revd. (New York: Charles Scribner's sons, 1954), bk. iii ch 1, p. 180.

76. David Carr, 'Spiritual Language and the Ethics of Redemption: A Reply to Jim Mackenzie, *Journal of Philosophy of Education*, vol. 33, no. 3 (November 1999), pp. 415-61.

qualities, teachers can both avoid any charge of proselytism and also encourage a stronger faith than the cloistered version of Christianity promoted in previous generations.

CONCLUSION

Forms far more Spacious

As noted in the Introduction to this volume, the endeavour to balance the secular and religious dimensions of cultural initiation and to clarify the place of religion in the civic space is not just an Irish concern. The early years of the twenty-first century have witnessed serious attempts in France to ensure an understanding of religion and an appreciation of the cultural achievement it has inspired in secular state schools from which all teaching of religion is excluded. This is because the French have come to learn that one disturbing consequence of *laïcité*, (the secular, civic neutrality that has been described as a French passion/ *passion française*[1]) is religious illiteracy. In the previous chapter I suggested that one consequence of the same exclusion of religion from schools in the United States has been the domination of religious discourse in the public sphere by the voices of unreasoning, sanctimonious righteousness.

The approach adopted by policy-makers in Norway, by contrast, strives to strike a balance between Lutheranism, Humanism and other faith-traditions in that country. The attitude to the country's Christian heritage is positive.

> The Christian faith and tradition constitute a deep current in our history – a heritage that unites us as a people across religious persuasions. It has imprinted itself on the norms, world view, concepts and art of the people. It bonds us to other peoples in the rhythm of the week and in common holidays, but is also an abiding presence in our national traits: in architecture and music, in style and conventions, in ideas, idioms and identity.[2]

1. See the series of articles entitled *Laïcité, Passsion Française*, edited by Marc Couty in *Le Monde de l'Éducation*, no. 246 (mars 1997), pp. 80-84.
2. The Royal Ministry of Education, Research and Church Affairs, (1997) *Core

The first chapter of the Norwegian document on the core curriculum, *Core Curriculum for Primary, Secondary and Adult Education in Norway*, is entitled 'The Spiritual Human Being' with the sub-headings 'Christian and Humanistic Values' and 'Cultural Heritage and Identity'. In the preamble, the document summarises the aims of education as enunciated in the country's Education Acts. The first of six essential aims is called 'Moral Outlook'. The first two of the seven aims in this section are to secure a 'Christian and ethical upbringing' and 'increased awareness and understanding of fundamental Christian values'.[3] The 'principal aims' of primary and lower secondary education are, 'with the understanding of and in cooperation with the home, [to] assist in providing pupils with a Christian and ethical upbringing'.[4] The aims of upper secondary schooling are to 'contribute to increased awareness and understanding of basic Christian and humanist values'.[5]

In the body of the document, these aims are given more content. Education 'shall be based on fundamental Christian and humanistic values' and support 'freedoms of faith, thought, speech and action' and serve to counter discrimination based on 'race, religion, nationality or position'.[6] It is claimed that 'Christian and humanistic values both demand and foster tolerance, providing room for other cultures and customs'.[7] The authors are not unmindful of the challenge involved in reconciling educational aims. The second of four 'seemingly contradictory aims' is identified as providing 'familiarity with our Christian and humanist heritage – *and* knowledge of and respect for other religions and faiths'.[8]

The Norwegian approach is based on an inclusiveness that is

Curriculum for Primary, Secondary and Adult Education in Norway (Oslo: National Centre for Educational Resources, 1997), p. 7.

3. Ibid., p. 2.
4. Ibid., inside front cover
5. Ibid., inside front cover
6. Ibid., p. 7.
7. Ibid.
8. Ibid., p. 39.

also reflected in the trend of Irish policy. Although the State no longer assumes an active role in the religious formation of citizens, religion remains salient in the civic space represented by schools. More generally, in the early years of this millennium, it seems to me that there are grounds for confidence about the place of religion in Irish culture. Great changes have indeed taken place in its profile and these have been ably traced in Louise Fuller's study of Irish Catholicism since 1950.[9] The volume has the provocative sub-title '*The Undoing of a Culture*' but, if a culture has been undone, it is a custodial culture, preoccupied by institutional considerations. The culture superseded is, as Dermot Lane puts it, that of the 'Counter Reformation Church' that 'flourished in Ireland, and elsewhere, up to the mid 1960s'.[10] This understanding of Church, writes Lane, was 'defensive, exclusivist, and introverted' and was given 'expression in claims like "outside the Church, there is no salvation" and "error has no rights".'[11]

This culture has very little in common with the inclusive vision of the Christian Gospel that is being articulated today by theologians like Dermot Lane and others. Consider also the work of Michael Drumm in recovering the spirit of Irish Christianity before its Romanisation in the nineteenth century.[12] In this context too I should mention the work of Donagh O'Shea whose writings give expression to an expansive, Christian spirituality that has the potential to enrich the life of anyone, believer or non-believer.[13] If in the past the faith was associated with a denial of the world, the spirit of contemporary theology in Ireland can

9. Louise Fuller, *Irish Catholicism since 1950: The Undoing of a Culture* (Dublin: Gill and Macmillan, 2004).

10. Dermot Lane, 'Afterword – The Expanding Horizons of Catholic Education', in *The Future of Religion in Irish Education,* eds. Pádraig Hogan and Kevin Williams, (Dublin: Veritas, 1997), p. 130.

11. Ibid.

12. Michael Drumm, *Passage to Pasch: Revisiting the Catholic Sacraments* (Dublin: The Columba Press, 1998).

13. See, for example, Donagh O'Shea, *I Remember Your Name in the Night* (Dublin and Mystic CT: Dominican Publications/Twenty-Third Publications, 1997) and *Go Down to the Potter's House: A Journey into Meditation* (Dublin: Dominican Publications, 1992).

be said to be contributing to what has been described as a *'réenchantement du monde'*, a re-enchantment or re-enchanting of the world, that is, a recovery, re-expression and re-presentation of its Christian dimension.[14]

A similar vision of the place of religion within human experience is also to be found articulated within philosophy of education, notably in some of the writings of Pádraig Hogan.

> Religion addresses the deepest yearnings of the human heart. It seeks to bear witness to a fathomless abundance of all that is beyond the impressive scope of the sciences to explain. That nothing can be said with certainty in this field, or demonstrated beyond rational doubt, provides sufficient reason for many to rule out religion from the worthwhile concerns of human experience. For others, however, this uncertainty has itself a pressing force; it is seen as a defining feature of what it means to be human....
>
> So consciousness of the difference between what the sciences can explain about the 'how' of things, and what remains inexplicable and mysterious about the 'why' has endured. And what is significant in this difference has been treasured not only by people in religious ministry, but also by those in all walks of life – not least teachers – in whom the poetic and spiritual evoke a deep response.[15]

What Bryan MacMahon, to whose work Hogan also draws attention, calls religion in 'forms far more spacious'[16] is also finding voice in literature. Let us consider two examples.

The first is 'Lipstick on the Host', a story by Aidan Mathews,

---

14. I have taken the expression *réenchantement du monde* from Catherine Maignant, 'Re-imagining Transcendence in the Global Village, *Engaging Modernity: Readings of Irish Politics, Culture and Literature at the Turn of the Century*, pp. 71-84, p. 82, eds., Michael Böss and Eamon Maher (Dublin: Veritas, 2003). In this article, Maignant also draws on the work of Michael Drumm.

15. Pádraig Hogan, 'Religion in Education and the Integrity of Teaching as a Practice: The Experience of Irish National Schools in Changing Times, Irish National Teachers' Organisation, *Teaching Religion in the Primary School: Issues and Challenges* (Dublin: Irish National Teachers' Organisation, 2003), p. 63.

16. Bryan McMahon, *The Master* (Dublin: Poolbeg, 1992), p. 100.

that tells of a woman teacher approaching middle age who comes to find fulfilment in a romantic relationship that ends tragically.[17] The incident referred to in the title occurs where the main character is reluctant to receive Communion while wearing lipstick and takes home the Host to consume it with the deepest reverence there, a reverence that Mathews communicates very powerfully. But in analysing the text with students I have to invite them to consider the ironic juxtaposition of deep faith with a personal life that does not reflect Church teaching on marriage. What makes the story an even more memorable metaphor of contemporary Ireland is that the Mass takes place on Ash Wednesday in a pre-fab oratory in a shopping centre and it is packed full of shoppers. An image of modern, busy 'consumerist' Ireland becomes an image of people at worship.

The second example is from a passage in prose written in the most poetic of language by Paul Durcan. In this passage, Durcan is writing about the funeral Mass for artist Tony O'Malley, celebrated by Father Tony O'Brien, and he succeeds in communicating the unconditional outreach of the sacrament of the Eucharist. At the Eucharist itself, the priest 'not only invited but encouraged, implored, yet in no way coerced, everyone, all four hundred of us'[18] to join in the Eucharist at the table of the Lord. Father O'Brien is described as standing there holding his arms in an embrace designed to encourage rather than to compel 'all our boats to come in, all our frail currachs' and to accept the invitation to join in the breaking of bread 'at the table of peace'.[19] And almost everyone in the large congregation of some four hundred souls from all walks of life responded to the priest's invitation to participate in the Lord's Supper.[20]

These 'forms more spacious' are also expressed in the generous, non-defensive openness of many clergy and religious. At a

17. Aidan Mathews, *Lipstick on the Host* (London: Vintage, 1998).
18. Paul Durcan, *Paul Durcan's Diary* (Dublin: New Island, 2003), p. 163.
19. Ibid.
20. I need hardly say that attendance at a funeral Mass does not imply any expectation of mourners that they receive Holy Communion. Nor do I claim that the incident above reflects Church teaching regarding the Eucharist.

Christmas Mass, a curate welcomed parishioners, visitors from outside the parish, visitors from other Christian and non-Christian faith-traditions and visitors who did not believe in God but who wanted to be part of the community's celebration of Christmas. A married couple I know, one of whom had previously been married, met the local parish priest socially and expressed their regret at being excluded from full participation in the sacramental life of the Church. In reply he simply said that the Church was a large place and it had room for everyone. At a Mass before Christmas, another parish priest urged parents of adult children whose lifestyles might not be compatible with Church teaching to invite the children to return to religious practice on the basis that the Church is theirs too.

This impulse is further reflected in the outreach of Christian ministry as unconditional, inclusive service to the whole community irrespective of religious affiliation. Here, for example, is a comment from a chaplain in a third level institute about his ministry to bereaved students, a ministry that takes him literally 'to the edge of the grave' in support of students.

> We have a unique role in dealing with bereavement and suicide. Because of our calling we walk that extra mile ... we go to the edge of the grave ... we stand at the foot of the cross with them.[21]

In referring to these attitudes as reflecting the tenor of contemporary Catholicism, I do not wish to appropriate to the Church a new monopoly over spiritual expression and practice. I agree with the finding by Tom Inglis[22] that Irish people have

21. I have taken this quotation from research by Pat O'Donnell on the role of the chaplain in the Institutes of Technology. See Pat O'Donnell, 'Emmaus Revisited: The Vision and Practice of Chaplaincy in Institutes of Technology', MA Dissertation, Mater Dei Institute of Education, Dublin City University, 2004, p. 35.

22. Tom Inglis, 'Catholic Church, Religious Capital and Symbolic Dominance' in *Engaging Modernity: Readings of Irish Politics, Culture and Literature at the Turn of the Century* (Dublin: Veritas, 2003), pp. 43-70, pp. 48 and 43, eds., Böss and. Maher. Inglis has written extensively on the sociological profile of the Catholic Church in Ireland. An interesting recent book on the subject is Vincent Twomey, *The End of Irish Catholicism* (Dublin: Veritas, 2003).

learned to find 'new ways' of meeting their spiritual needs and that they 'do not think more or less of others for being or not being a good Catholic'.[22] Yet I do want to affirm the enduring profile in Irish life of the Christian faith that continues to inspire so many Irish women and men. This is indeed the faith that many commentators throughout history have perceived as an Irish passion.[23] And, as noted earlier in respect of current work in theology, this faith too is finding 'new ways' and new languages in which to express its timeless truths.[24] Its role in the civic space is no longer based on expediency or in mere compliance with a cultural norm but rather derives from the place of religious commitment in the heart and minds of the people of Ireland.

23. This perception of Irish religious commitment emerges from sources quoted in two of the texts that I have drawn on for some of the historical references in this book: Louise Fuller, *Irish Catholicism Since 1950: The Undoing of a Culture* (Dublin: Gill and Macmillan, 2004) and Colm Lennon, *Sixteenth Century Ireland: The Incomplete Conquest* (Dublin: Gill and Macmillan, 1994).

24. I would refer readers once more to the work of Michael Drumm in recovering traditional expressions of Irish Christianity that articulate 'the mystery of Christ's pasch ... in *communitas* with the earth, with the dead and with all people who continue on the journey from passage to pasch', Drumm, *Passage to Pasch,* p. 143.

Bibliography

Achebe, Chinua. *Things Fall Apart*. London: Heinemann,1986.

Alexander, Hanan and McLaughlin, T. H., 'Education in Religion and Spirituality'. In *The Blackwell Guide to Philosophy of Education*, pp. 356-73. Edited by Nigel Blake; Paul Smeyers; Richard Smith; and Paul Standish. Oxford: Blackwell, 2003.

Allende, Isabel. *My Invented Country: A Memoir*. London: Harper Perennial, 2004.

Allott, Kenneth, ed. *The Penguin Book of Contemporary Verse*. London: Penguin, 1968.

Alvey, David. *Irish Education: The Case for Secular Reform*. Dublin and Belfast: Church and StateBooks/Athol Books, 1992.

Association of Community Schools. Model Lease for Community Schools. Dublin: Association of Community Schools, 1992.

Bennett, Jackie and Forgan, Rosemary, eds. *Convent Girls*. London: Virago Press, 2003.

Bennett, James. 'Changing Values in Primary Education', *Studies: An Irish Quarterly Review*, vol. 84, no. 333 (1995), pp. 71-9.

Bloom, Harold. *How to Read and Why*. London: Fourth Estate, 2001.

Bost, Alain. *La Fin de l'État Laïc, Le Monde de L'Éducation*, no. 306 (septembre 2002), p. 6.

Bourke, Jackie. 'Ye of Little Faith', *The Irish Times: Education and Living Supplement*. 3 February 1998, p. 5.

Bradley, Bruce. 'Ghostly Rhythms: Philosophy and Religion in Irish Education, *Studies: An Irish Quarterly Review*, vol. 83, no. 330 (1994), pp. 143-52.

Campaign to Separate Church and State Ltd and Jeremiah Noel Murphy v Minister for Education, the Attorney General, The Most Reverend Cathal Daly, The Most Reverend Desmond Connell, The Most Reverend Dermot Clifford and the Most Reverend Joseph Cassidy: Supreme Court 1996 No. 36, Hamilton CJ. O'Flaherty, Denham, Barrington and Keane JJ, 25 March 1998. *Irish Law Review Monthly*, 2 1998, pp. 81-101.

Carr, David, and Haldane, John, eds. *Spirituality, Philosophy and Education*. London: RoutledgeFalmer, 2003.

Carr, David. 'Spiritual Language and the Ethics of Redemption: A Reply to Jim Mackenzie, *Journal of Philosophy of Education*, vol. 33, no. 3 (November 1999), pp. 415-461.

Cédelle, Luc. *Parler Religion en Toute Laïcité, Le Monde de L'Éducation*, 321 (janvier 2004), pp. 30-32.

Claus, Hugo. *The Sorrow of Belgium,* translated by Arnold J. Pomerans. Woodstock and New York: The Overlook Press, 2002.

Comhlucht Oideachais, An. *An Scealaí,* Céime 3, Leabhar B, Duilleoga. Baile Atha Cliath: An Comhlucht Oideachais, 1989.

Congregation for Catholic Education. *The Religious Dimension of Education in a Catholic School: Guidelines for Reflection and Renewal.* London: Catholic Truth Society, 1988.

Convention Secretariat, The, Coolahan, J., ed. *Report on the National Education Convention.* Dublin: The Stationery Office, 1994.

Coolahan, John. 'Curricular Policy for the Primary and Secondary Schools of Ireland 1900 - 35'. Ph. D. dissertation, Dublin University, 1973.

Couty, Marc. *Laïcité, Passsion Française, Le Monde de l'Éducation,* no. 246 (mars 1997), pp. 80-84.

Cowan, James. *A Mapmaker's Dream.* New York: Warners Books, 1986,

Craig, Patricia, ed. *The Oxford Book of Ireland.* Oxford: Oxford University Press, 1999.

De Loo, Tessa. *The Twins.* London: Arcadia, 2001.

De Valera, Eamonn. Radio broadcast 17 March 1943. http://www.searcs-web.com/dev.html. Accessed 10 July 2004.

Debray, Régis. *L'Enseignement du Fait Religieux dans L'École Laïque.* Paris: Editions Odile Jacob, 2002..

Department of Education. *Memorandum V. 40: Organisation of Whole-time Continuation Courses in Borough, Urban and County Areas, 1942.* Dublin: Department of Education, 1942.

Department of Education and Science. *Junior Certificate: Religious Education Syllabus: Ordinary and Higher Level.* Dublin: The Stationery Office, 2000.

——. Key Statistics about the Department's Customers, on the department's website http://www.education.ie Accessed 25 March 2004.

——. *Primary School Curriculum Geography.* Dublin: The Stationery Office, 1999.

——. *Primary School Curriculum History.* Dublin: The Stationery Office, 1999.

——. *The Primary Curriculum: Introduction.* Dublin: The Stationery Office, 1999.

Department of Education. 'Notes for Teachers – Irish'. Dublin: The Stationery Office, 1933.

——. *Memorandum V. 40: Organisation of Whole-time Continuation Courses in Borough, Urban and County Areas, 1942.* Dublin: Department of Education, 1942.

——. 'Notes on the Teaching of Civics'. Dublin: Department of Education, 1966.

——. Circular Letter M4/95: Relationships and Sexuality Education. Dublin: Department of Education, 1995.

——. Circular letter No. 7/79: Religious Instruction in Vocational

Schools. Dublin: Department of Education, 1979.

———. *Curraclam na Bunscoile: Lámhleabhar an Oide/Primary School Curriculum: Teacher's Handbook* : *Parts One and Two.* Dublin: The Stationery Office, 1971.

———. *Rules for National Schools under the Department of Education.* Dublin: The Stationery Office, 1965.

———. *The Junior Certificate: Civic, Social and Political Education Syllabus.* Dublin: The Stationery Office, 1996.

Donoghue, Denis. *The Practice of Reading.* New Haven and London: Yale University Press, 1998.

Doyle, Roddy. *A Star Called Henry.* London: Jonathan Cape, 1999.

———. 'Republic Is a Beautiful Word'. In *My Favourite Year: A Collection of New Football Writing,* pp. 7-21. Edited by Nick Hornby. London: H., F. and G. Witherby, 1993.

Drumm, Michael. *Passage to Pasch: Revisiting the Catholic Sacraments.* Dublin: The Columba Press, 1998.

Dunne, Joseph, 'The Catholic School and Civil Society: Exploring the Tensions'. In *The Catholic School in Contemporary Society,* pp.18-46. Conference of Major Religious Superiors. Dublin: Conference of Major Religious Superiors, 1991,

Durcan, Paul. *Paul Durcan's Diary.* Dublin: New Island, 2003.

Educate Together. *Learn Together: An Ethical Education Curriculum for Educate Together Schools.* Dublin: Educate Together, 2004.

Eileen Flynn v Sister Anna Power and the Sisters of the Holy Faith: High Court Circuit Court Appeal Costello J., 8 March 1985. Irish Law Review Monthly (1985), pp. 336-343.

Fallon, C. J. *The Crock of Gold,* Stage 4, book 2, Rainbow Reading Programme. Dublin: Fallons, 1984.

Forna, Aminatta. *The Devil that Danced on the Water.* London: Flamingo, 2003.

Fuller, Louise. *Irish Catholicism Since 1950: The Undoing of a Culture.* Dublin: Gill and Macmillan, 2004.

Gold, Karen. 'Faith in Our Schools', *Guardian Education,* 25 April 2000, pp. 2-3.

Government of Ireland. *Bunreacht na hÉireann/Constitution of Ireland.* Dublin: The Stationery Office, 1937/1990.

———. *Charting Our Education Future: White Paper on Education.* Dublin: The Stationery Office, 1995.

———. *Education Act 1998.* Dublin: The Stationery Office, 1998.

———. *Education for A Changing World: Green Paper on Education.* Dublin: The Stationery Office, 1992.

———. *Employment Equality Act 1998.* Dublin: The Stationery Office, 1998.

———. *Employment Equality Bill 1996.* Dublin: The Stationery Office, 1996.

———. *Equal Status Act 2000.* Dublin: The Stationery Office, 2000.

Government of Ireland/Department of Education, *The Junior Certificate: Civic, Social and Political Education Syllabus.* Dublin: The Stationery

Office, 1996.

Hoffman, Eva. *Lost In Translation: A Life in a New Language.* London: Vintage, 1998.

Hogan Pádraig and Williams, Kevin, eds. *The Future of Religion in Irish Education.* Dublin: Veritas, 1997.

Hogan, Pádraig. 'Religion in Education and the Integrity of Teaching as a Practice: The Experience of Irish National Schools in Changing Times'. In *Teaching Religion in the Primary School: Issues and Challenges,* pp.63-74. Irish National Teachers' Organisation, Dublin: Irish National Teachers' Organisation, 2003.

Howard, Jason, J. 'Interview with William Desmond', *The Leuven Philosophy Newsletter,* Vol. 2 (2002), pp. 15-19.

Hyland Áine and Milne, Kenneth, eds. *Irish Educational Documents,* Vol. 1. Dublin: The Church of Ireland College of Education, 1987.

——. *Irish Educational Documents,* Vol II. Dublin: The Church of Ireland College of Education, 1992.

Inglis, Tom. 'Catholic Church, Religious Capital and Symbolic Dominance'. In *Engaging Modernity: Readings of Irish Politics, Culture and Literature at the Turn of the Century,* pp. 43-70. Edited by Michael Böss and Eamon Maher. Dublin: Veritas, 2003,.

Irish National Teachers' Organisation. 'Open Forum'. In *Teaching Religion in the Primary School: Issues and Challenges,* pp. 85-101. Irish National Teachers' Organisation. Dublin: Irish National Teachers' Organisation, 2003.

——. *Primary School Curriculum: An Evolutionary Process.* Dublin: Irish National Teachers' Organisation, 1996.

——. *Teaching Religion in the Primary School: Issues and Challenges.* Dublin: Irish National Teachers' Organisation, 2003.

Johnson, Richard. 'The Schooling of the English Working-Class, 1780-1850', In *Schooling and Capitalism,* pp. 44-54. Edited by Roger Dale; Geoff Esland; and Madeleine MacDonald. London and Henley: Routledge and Kegan Paul/Open University Press, 1976.

Judge, Harry. *Faith-based Schools and the State: Catholics in America, France and England.* Oxford: Symposium Book, 2002.

Kant, Immanuel, *Prolegomena to Any Future Metaphysics.* New York: MacMillan, 1950.

Kellaghan, Thomas; McGee, Páid; Millar, David; Perkins, Rachel. Views of the Irish Public on Education: 2004 Survey. Dublin: Educational Research Centre. http://www.education.ie/servlet/blobservlet/yes_survey_report.pdf.

Kelly, John M. *The Irish Constitution.* Edited by G. Hogan and G. Whyte fourth edition. Dublin: LexisNexis, 2003.

Kerrigan, Gene. *Another Country: Growing up in '50s Ireland.* Dublin: Gill and Macmillan, 1998.

Kiberd, Declan. *Inventing Ireland: The Literature of the Modern Nation.* London: Vintage, 1996.

Kieran, Patricia. 'Promoting Truth? Inter-Faith Education in Irish Catholic Primary Schools'. In *Teaching Religion in the Primary School: Issues and Challenges*, pp.119-130. Irish National Teachers' Organisation. Dublin: Irish National Teachers' Organisation, 2003.

Kingsolver, Barbara. *The Poisonwood Bible*. London, Faber and Faber, 1999.

Kjeldsen, Busk, Madsen and Pedersen v. Denmark, European Court of Human Rights, 1976. European Human Rights Reports, Series A, No. 23 (1976), pp. 711-736.

Lane, Dermot A. 'Afterword – The Expanding Horizons of Catholic Education'. In *The Future of Religion in Irish Education*, pp. 128-137. Edited by Pádraig Hogan and Kevin Williams. Dublin: Veritas, 1997.

Lennon Colm. *Sixteenth Century Ireland: The Incomplete Conquest*. Dublin: Gill and Macmillan, 1994.

Lomasky, Loren. *Persons, Rights and the Moral Community*. New York: Oxford University Press, 1987.

McCarthy, Mary. *Memories of a Catholic Girlhood*. Harmondworth, London: Penguin, 1967.

McEwan, Ian. *The Child in Time*. London: Picador, 1988.

McGahern, John. *That They May Face the Rising Sun*. London: Faber and Faber, 2003.

McGrady, Andrew G. 'The Religious Dimension of Education in Irish Second Level Schools at the Start of the Third Millennium', *REA/ Religion, Education and the Arts*, vol. 4 (2003), pp. 53-87.

Mackenzie, Jim. 'David Carr on Religious Knowledge and Spiritual Education', *Journal of Philosophy of Education*, vol. 32, no. 3 (November 1998), pp. 409-427.

McMahon, Bryan. *The Master* Dublin: Poolbeg, 1992.

McSweeney, Siobhán. 'The Poets' Picture of Education', *The Crane Bag*, vol. 7, no. 2 (1983), pp. 134-142.

Maher, Eamon. 'An Interview with John McGahern: Catholicism and National Identity in the Works of John McGahern', *Studies: An Irish Quarterly Review*, vol. 90, no. 357, (Spring 2001), pp. 70-83.

Maignant, Catherine. 'Re-imagining Transcendence in the Global Village'. In *Engaging Modernity: Readings of Irish Politics, Culture and Literature at the Turn of the Century*, pp. 71-84. Edited by Michael Böss and Eamon. Maher. Dublin: Veritas, 2003.

Martin, Augustine, ed., *Soundings: Leaving Certificate Poetry Interim Anthology*. Dublin: Gill and Macmillan, Longmans, Browne and Nolan, 1969.

Mill, John Stuart. *On Liberty*. In *Mill*, Norton Critical Edition. Edited by Alan Ryan. New York/London: W.W. Norton, 1997.

Murphy, Christina. 'Question and Answer', *The Irish Times: Education and Living Supplement,* 9 May 1995, p. 9.

——. 'Q and A/Question and Answer', *The Irish Times: Education and Living Supplement,* 29 September 1995, p. 9.

Murphy, Daniel. *Education and the Arts*. Dublin: School of Education, Trinity College, Dublin, 1987.

Nafisi, Azar. *Reading Lolita in Tehran: A Memoir in Books*. London and New York: Fourth Estate, 2004.

National Programme Conference, The. *Report and Programme*. Dublin: The Stationery Office, 1926/26.

New Schools Advisory Committee. Public Consultation on Proposed New Primary Schools for September 2005. Tullamore: Department of Education and Science, 2004.

Norman, James. *Ethos and Education*. New York: Peter Lang, 2003.

Oakeshott, Michael. *On Human Conduct*. Oxford: Clarendon Press, 1975.

O'Connor, Fionnuala. *A Shared Childhood: The Story of Integrated Schools in Northern Ireland*. Belfast: Blackstaff Press, 2002.

O'Donnell, Pat. 'Emmaus Revisited: The Vision and Practice of Chaplaincy in Institutes of Technology', MA Dissertation, Mater Dei Institute of Education, Dublin City University, 2004.

O'Leary, Olivia. *Politicians and Other Animals*. Dublin: The O'Brien Press, 2004.

O'Shea, Donagh. *Go Down to the Potter's House: A Journey into Meditation*. Dublin: Dominican Publications, 1992.

——. *I Remember Your Name in the Night*. Dublin and Mystic CT: Dominican Publications/Twenty-Third Publications, 1997.

Parks, Tim. *An Italian Education*. London: Vintage, 2000.

Pollack, Andy. 'New School Curriculum Leaves out God in Favour of Spiritual Dimension', *The Irish Times* 22 August 1998, p. 4.

Raffi, Guy. '*Le Nouveau Combat des Laïques*', *Le Monde de l'Éducation*, no. 246 (mars 1997), pp. 83-84.

Reener-Tauch, Roberta/Killeen, John. *Let's Go*: Stage 4, Book 2. Dublin: Gill and Macmillan, 1983.

Rosenblith, Suzanne, Priestman, Scott. 'Problematizing Religious Truth: Implications for Public Education'. *Educational Theory*, vol. 54, no. 4 (2004), pp. 365-380.

Rowe, Paul. 'Inclusive Schools Need More Support', *The Irish Times*, 4 October 2004, p. 14.

Royal Ministry of Education, Research and Church Affairs, The. *Core Curriculum for Primary, Secondary and Adult Education in Norway*. Oslo: National Centre for Educational Resources, 1997.

Russell, Mary. 'Lost and Found Land', *The Irish Times Magazine*, 15 March 2003, pp. 14-15.

Sandsmark, Signe. *Is World View Neutral Education Possible and Desirable?* Carlisle: Paternoster Press, 2000.

Tomasevski, Katarina. *Human Rights in Education as a Prerequisite for Human Rights Education: Right to Education Primer No. 4*. Gotenburg: Swedish International Development Cooperation Agency, 2001. http://www.right-to-education.org/content/primers/rte_04.pdf.

Accessed 30 March 2004.

Tovey, Hilary and Share, Perry. *A Sociology of Ireland,* second edition. Dublin: Gill and Macmillan, 2003.

Truong, Nicolas. '*Enseigner les Religions: Chassé-Croisé Européen*', *Le Monde de L'Éducation,* no. 306 (septembre 2002), pp. 76-78.

Twomey, Vincent. *The End of Irish Catholicism.* Dublin: Veritas, 2003.

Uí Mhaonaile, Siobhán. 'Interdenominational Schools', Letters to the Editor. *The Irish Times,* 30 April 2002, p. 15.

Walshe, John. 'Minister Being Forced to Tackle Risky Issue of Religion in Schools'. *The Irish Times,* 12 November, 1991, p. 10.

Walsh, P.D. *Education and Meaning: Philosophy in Practice.* London: Cassell, 1993.

Whitehead, A. N., *Religion in the Making.* Cambridge: Cambridge University Press, 1926.

Williams, Kevin. 'Reason and Rhetoric in Curriculum Policy: An Appraisal of the Case for the Inclusion of Irish in the School Curriculum', *Studies: An Irish Quarterly Review,* vol. 78, no. 310 (1989) pp. 191-203.

——. 'Public Funds and Minority Broadcasting', In *The Media and the Marketplace: Ethical Perspectives,* pp. 33-44. Edited by Eoin G. Cassidy and Andrew G. McGrady. Dublin: Institute of Public Administration, 2001.

——. The Religious Dimension of Cultural Initiation: Has It a Place in a Secular World?', *Ethical Perspectives,* vol. 11, no. 4 (December 2004), pp. 228-237.